THE BOOK OF CLEAN JOKES

Toni Sortor

**Exclusively distributed by
P.S.I. & Associates, Inc.
13322 S.W. 128th Street
Miami, Florida 33186
Phone (305) 255-7959**

ISBN 1-55748-081-8

Printed in the United States of America

The Book of Clean Jokes

Contents

Contents

Contents

Advertising

When the United States attacked Libya in April of 1986, some newspapers carried an Associated Press picture of a Navy jet fighter flying above the Mediterranean off the Libyan coast. In the window of the plane was a sign: **Send Cookies.**

John D. Gavin, a retired rear admiral, and Frank Gibbs, a retired executive of the Winn-Dixie grocery chain, led a drive that resulted in one hundred cases of cookies being sent to the crew of the USS *Saratoga*.

-John Bohannon

*

Malcolm G. Krebbs was the last of the old diehards who believed in doing business without advertising, and like so many others he found that his philosophy just didn't work anymore. So he finally went to an advertising agency, but with great misgivings. Mr. Krebbs just couldn't manage to understand the principle behind advertising until his account executive explained it to him like this: Doing business without advertising is like winking at a girl in the dark; you know what you are doing, but nobody else does.

-George Jessel

*

Did you hear about that brand-new deodorant called Invisible? You apply it, and it makes you disappear. Then everyone wonders where that peculiar odor is coming from.

-George Jessel

*

With great pride, Benjamin Bernstein painted himself a sign to hang over his store: FRESH FISH SOLD HERE DAILY

As Bernstein placed the ladder to hang up the sign, a kibitzer sang out, "What kind of cockamamy sign is that?"

"Why? What's wrong with it?"

"*Fresh* fish, Bernstein? It would never occur to your customers that you sell fish that *aren't* fresh — unless you advertise it!"

"You're right." Bernstein took his brush and painted out "Fresh."

"Wait!" said the kibitzer. "What about 'Sold'? Obviously you sell fish; you don't give them away free."

Mr. Bernstein painted out "Sold," and said, "O.K.?"

"No. Why 'Here'? Obviously, you don't sell fish over *there*."

"You're right!" And Bernstein painted out "Here."

"That leaves 'Daily,' " said the kibitzer. "I ask you, is that smart? If fish are fresh they *must* come in and go out daily. Right?"

"Absolutely!" Bernstein crossed out "Daily," leaving a sign that read only: FISH

"Perfect," said the kibitzer.

Now Bernstein started up the ladder, when along came another kibitzer.

"Why are you putting up that ridiculous sign?"

"What's wrong with it?"

"You don't have to put up any signs, Bernstein. *Your* fish everyone smells a mile away!"

So Bernstein put up no sign at all, thinking how lucky he was to have friends of such uncommon acumen.

-Leo Rosten

*

No wonder our country's having trouble with its allies. They're all worried about Communism, nuclear war, starvation, and drought. What are we worried about? Underarm odor!

Age

At twenty we don't care what the world thinks of us; at thirty we worry about what it thinks of us; at sixty we discover that it wasn't even thinking of us.

-Sam Levenson

*

Life begins at forty, but so does arthritis and the habit of telling the same story three times to the same person.

-Sam Levenson

*

The housefly, escorting her daughter across the head of a completely bald man, observed, "How quickly times change! When I was your age, my dear, this was just a footpath."

*

The old codger was being interviewed on his one-hundredth birthday. "I'm proud to say I haven't an enemy in the world," he boasted.

"That's a wonderful thought," said the young reporter.

"Sure is," the old man said with a smile. "Outlived every blamed one of them!"

Animals

Frank Bacon retired after thirty-four years as a mailman. And he claimed to hold the record for being bitten by dogs: twenty-three times.

On Bacon's last day at work, his supervisors came up with a cute publicity picture. They had Bacon hold three adorable puppies in his arms. One of them bit him.

-John Bohannon

*

What's long and green and goes "hith, hith"? A snake with a lisp.

-Michael Johnstone

*

What would you call a bad-tempered gorilla with cotton wool in his ears? Anything you want. He can't hear you.

-Michael Johnstone

*

What's the best way to get five elephants in a subcompact? Two in the front, two in the back, and one in the glove compartment.

-Michael Johnstone

*

What's the difference between and elephant and spaghetti? Elephants don't slip off the end of your fork.

-Michael Johnstone

*

What do you get if you cross a flat fish with George Washington?
The flounder of our country.

-Michael Johnstone

*

What do you get if you cross a skunk with an eagle? An animal that stinks to high heaven.

-Michael Johnstone

*

Epitaph on the gravestone of an army mule: Here lies Maggie, who in her time kicked two colonels, four majors, ten captains, twenty-four lieutenants, forty-two sergeants, four hundred eighty-six privates, and one bomb.

*

A lion was stalking through the jungle one day when he came across a bull. The lion and the bull got into a tremendous battle, but in the end the lion killed the bull and ate him up. The lion was so pleased with himself that he threw back his head and roared and roared. The noise attracted a hunter who followed the sound until he found the lion. The hunter took aim and killed the lion with a single shot.

Moral : When you are full of bull, it's wise to keep your mouth shut.

-George Jessel

*

A man was driving through a small, seemingly deserted town when suddenly he came upon a huge crowd of people gathered in front of the town hall. His curiosity got the best of him, so he parked his car and joined the crowd.

"What's going on?" he inquired of one of the townspeople.

"Ned Blacker's mule kicked his mother-in-law in the head and killed her," was the reply.

"Oh, then this is a memorial service?"

"No, this here's an auction. Every man in town wants to buy that mule!"

-George Jessel

*

What do you get if you cross an elephant with a mouse? Enormous holes in the baseboard.

-Michael Johnstone

*

What do you get if you cross an elephant with a crow? Lots of broken telephone poles.

-Michael Johnstone

*

What's black and white and makes a horrible noise? A penguin playing the bagpipes.

-Michael Johnstone

*

What do you get if you cross a mynah bird with a lion? I don't know, but if it speaks to you, you'd better listen!

-Michael Johnstone

*

The Scotchman was visiting a relative in Maine. One evening, he pointed into the woods and asked, "What's that animal?"

"Oh, that's a moose," his relative said.

"A moose? Well, if that's an American moose, I hope I never meet one of your rats!"

*

A pig walks into a Western Union office, takes a telegram blank, and writes: Oink Oink Oink Oink Oink Oink Oink Oink Oink.

The clerk looks at the telegram and says, "But that's only nine words. You can put in another Oink for the same price."

The pig looks at him in disgust and says, "But then it wouldn't make any sense!"

*

What do you call a dog that has no legs? Don't bother. It won't come, anyway.

*

What do you do each morning with a dog that has no legs? Take it out for a drag.

*

The city slicker was stuck right behind an old truck on the way to market with a load of hogs. Suddenly, one hog jumped ship, just missed being hit by the city slicker, and took off into a field. The man got out of his car, chased the hog, eventually caught him, and bullied him into the backseat of his car. Then he set off after the old truck, which was now out of sight.

As he went whipping along, a policeman pulled him over. "Officer, I'm trying to catch the truck this hog jumped out of," he replied.

"You'll never catch that truck now," the officer said. "Just take the hog to the zoo."

The next day, the officer saw the car again, with the hog still in the backseat. He pulled the man over and said, "I thought I told you to take that hog to the zoo yesterday."

"I did, officer," the man replied. "We had such a great time that today we're going to the beach!"

*

What goes 999-thump, 999-thump? A centipede with a wooden leg.

*

Why did Snoopy quit his job? He got tired of working for Peanuts.

*

What could possibly be smarter than a talking horse? A spelling bee.

*

What do you get when you cross an elephant with a computer? A two-ton know-it-all.

*

"Where's everyone going?" one chicken asked another as they ran along with the flock.

"The farmer said some men were going to lay a sidewalk out front, and we all want to see how they do it."

*

First fish: I've been in schools all my life.

Second fish: Really think you're smart, don't you? Listen, you may be educated, but my ancestors swam under the *Mayflower*.

*

Armed Forces

A clerk at this U.S. Army base filled out a requisition order form for a headlight costing six dollars. Following procedure, he used the base's computer system and punched in an eleven-digit code number. One digit was incorrect, but the military supply clerk at the other end didn't know it, because the order carried no description, just the item number. So he sent back a seven-ton ship's anchor costing $28,560.

No one questioned why an army base a thousand miles from the nearest ocean would need an anchor. Army officials kept the anchor for a few weeks, hoping that some other branch of the service might need it. But there were no takers. Apparently the Navy had all the anchors it needed. So the Army shipped the anchor to the Pueblo Army Depot, about forty miles away, for storage.

-John Bohannon

*

An African dictator was invited to inspect his air force's new amphibious aircraft. He piloted it himself, and everything went fine until he prepared to land at the airport.

"Excuse me, Sir," said his nervous copilot, "but it would be better to land on the lake, since the plane has pontoons."

The dictator swung the plane out over the lake and made a fair landing. Rising from his seat, he thanked his nervous copilot for his tact in avoiding a horrible mistake, opened the door, and stepped straight into the lake.

*

Horses were valuable and scarce during the American Revolution, and a young officer had been sent out to confiscate any stock he could find in a certain area of Virginia. He came to a fine old mansion where he saw a team of horses working a field. Knocking on the door, he informed the dignified older woman of the house that he was confiscating her team.

"I need them for spring plowing," she complained.

"I'm sorry, but those are my commander's orders," the officer replied firmly.

"And who is your commander, young man?"

"General George Washington, commander-in-chief of the American army," the officer said with some pride.

The lady allowed herself a little smile as she said, "You go back and tell George that his mother will not let him have her horses."

*

An army barber was just finishing cutting the draftee's hair. "Like to keep these sideburns of yours?" he asked solicitously. The draftee answered fervently, "I sure would!"

"Okay," chirped the barber. "Catch!"

-Bennett Cerf

*

A scientist invented a salve that could bring inanimate objects to life, so he tried it out on the statue of a great general. Sure enough, the statue gave a quiver and a moment later the general, creaking a bit in the joints, climbed down from his pedestal.

The scientist was overjoyed. "I have given you back your life," he exulted. "Now tell me, General, what's the first thing you are going to do with it?"

"That's easy," rasped the general, ripping his gun from his holster. "I'm going to shoot me about two million pigeons!"

*

"Listen, boys," the tough sergeant told his men before they went into battle, "we've got the best medical team in the world working for us. If you're hit, they'll take care of you, so don't worry."

"Sarge? When you get hit, how do you know whether you're dead or alive?" asked a young voice from the back of the group.

"That's easy. If you're hungry and your feet are cold, you're alive."

"How do you figure that?"

"Well, if you're hungry, you can be sure you're not in heaven. And if your feet are cold, you sure aren't in hell!"

*

Did you know that all military doctors are officers? Except for the one that handed a general a thermometer and told him exactly what to do with it.

*

The Afghanistans claimed the Russians were using poison gas on them. Maybe, but it's more likely that the wind just changed and blew the exhaust from the Russian army's kitchens their way.

*

Did you hear about the new Israeli weapon? It's a huge gun that fires two-week-old bagels. If one of them misses you, the lox still gags you.

*

The drill sergeant was chewing out a new recruit. "Tell me, dummy, what would happen if one of your ears were shot off?"

"I couldn't hear, Sarge."

"That's right. What if both your ears were shot off?"

"I couldn't see."

"You couldn't see? How do you figure that, dummy?"

"If both my ears were shot off, Sarge, my helmet would slide down right over my eyes!"

*

During a training exercise, a very young captain sideswiped his admiral's flagship and raced away from the scene of the accident. Minutes later, the admiral sent the young captain an urgent message: "What do you intend to do now?"

The captain sent back this reply: "Buy a farm!"

*

The recruit returned to the supply officer just a few minutes after being issued his uniform.

"What're you doing back here?" the officer barked. "I suppose you're going to claim that uniform doesn't fit?"

"Well, it's like this, sir," the recruit stammered. "The shirt and jacket fit just fine...."

"So?"

"But the pants are a little loose around the armpits, sir."

*

During World War I, a young American officer was on patrol when a young English officer approached. "Who are you?" the American demanded.

"The Prince of Wales," was the reply.

"Sure. And I'm the king of England!"

Several days later, the American attended a social event where the Prince of Wales was introduced. As the American attempted to disappear into the woodwork, the prince waved to him from across the room and called out cheerfully, "Hello there, Dad!"

*

An American, visiting Israel, was invited to the ceremonies dedicating the Tomb of the Unknown Soldier.

Speeches were made by the president of Israel, by Ben-Gurion, by the commanding general of the army, and at last the tarpaulin that covered the monument was pulled aside — to reveal a simple, marble plinth, on front of which was engraved: Chaim Isadore Cohn, Born, Poland, 1903, Died, Israel, 1955.

"I thought this was a tomb to the unknown soldier!" exclaimed the American.

"Oh, it is," said the Israeli.

"But how? Unknown? They've inscribed his name, his birthdate, his...."

"Ah," said the Israeli, "you don't understand. As a *tailor*, he was known; but as a soldier — *mneh*!

-Leo Rosten

*

Business

A lady sent the following letter to a mail-order house: "Gentlemen: Please send me the frying pan on page ten of your catalog. If it's any good, I'll send you $14.95 by return mail."

The reply came back: "Madam: Please send us your check for $14.95. If it's any good, we'll send you the frying pan by return mail."

*

A collection letter that's producing gratifying results has been devised by an ingenious retailer. It's supposedly a two-page letter, but the first page is missing. The top of the second page (the one that's actually sent) reads, "We're sure you don't want us to do that to you, *do you?*"

-Bennett Cerf

*

Two traveling salesmen were unable to obtain separate rooms in a busy hotel one night, so they reluctantly agreed to share a king-sized bed.

"I won't sleep a wink all night," moaned the first.

"Me, either," agreed the second as he turned out the light.

Early the next morning, the first asked the second, "Did you sleep?"

"Not at all. I heard every noise."

"Me, too."

As they struggled to leave the bed, they saw it was covered with plaster. The ceiling had fallen on them during the night, but neither had heard a thing — and they had insomnia!

*

You know why workers in Japan are so productive and obedient? When they fire you over there, you get a pink slip *and* a sword.

Children

The young lad struggled out of the small lake, fully clothed and dripping. A kindly passerby stopped to give him a hand, and then said, "But how did you come to fall in, my boy?" The boy allowed an expression of contempt to cross his face and said, "I didn't come to fall in! I came to fish."

*

A farmer gathered his six sons around him to demand, "Which one of you boys pushed the outhouse into the creek?" The culprit did not step forward. "Now, boys," said the farmer, "remember the story of George Washington and the cherry tree. It's true that young George chopped down that tree, but he told his father the truth, and his father was proud of him." Whereupon the farmer's youngest son stepped forward and admitted that he had pushed the outhouse into the creek. The farmer picked up a switch and whipped his son soundly.

"But Pa," protested the boy tearfully, "you told me that George Washington's father was *proud* of him when he confessed to chopping down the cherry tree."

"He was, son," replied the farmer, "but George Washington's father wasn't *sitting* in the cherry tree when his son chopped it down!"

-George Jessel

*

Permissiveness believes in letting your child do whatever he likes on the premise that if he gets killed doing it, he won't do it again.

-Sam Levenson

*

Somewhere on this globe, every ten seconds, there is a woman giving birth to a child. She must be found and stopped!

-Sam Levenson

*

What's the best way to stop children from jumping up and down in bed? Put Crazy Glue on the ceiling.

-Michael Johnstone

*

As punishment for her previously bad table manners, the little girl was being forced to eat her dinner on a card table set up in the corner of the dining room. The rest of the family ignored her until she said grace over her lonely meal: "Thank You, Lord, for preparing a table before me in the presence of my enemies."

*

Two men sank into adjacent train seats after a long day in the city. One asked the other, "Your son go back to college yet?"

"Yeah. He left yesterday. Yours?"

"Two days ago."

"Hm. Mine's a senior this year, so it's almost over. In May, he'll be an engineer. What's your boy going to be when he gets out of college?"

"At the rate he's going, I'd say he'll be about thirty."

"No, I mean what's he taking in college?"

"He's taking every penny I make."

"Doesn't he burn the midnight oil enough?"

"He doesn't get in early enough to burn the midnight oil."

"Well, has sending him to college done anything at all?"

"Sure has! It's totally cured his mother of bragging about him!"

*

The teacher looked at the new student. "Please introduce yourself to the class," she said kindly.

My name is Iglethorpe Mohhandas Friplesnerf."

"How do you spell that?"

"My mother helps me."

*

Do you know that quintuplets only happen about once out of 50 million times? What I want to know is, when do those women find time to do any housework?

*

Dad had decided it was time to talk to his son about the future. "What do you want to do with your life, boy? Do you want to be a doctor, lawyer, or what?"

"No. None of those, dad. I want to drive one of those huge army tanks."

"Well, if that's what you want to do, I certainly won't stand in your way!"

*

"Junior, if you eat one more piece of pie, you'll burst!"

"I know. Pass the pie and stand back!"

*

"Mom!" Junior yelled. "Come quick! There's a bear in our yard!"

Out of breath and scared to death, Junior's mother looked out the window. "Junior, that's just Harold's dog. Go to your room and ask God to forgive you for lying and scaring me so."

A few minutes later, Junior reappeared.

"Did you ask God to forgive you?"

"Yes. He said it was okay. The first time He saw Harold's dog, He thought it was a bear, too."

*

Two neighbors chatting by the fence noticed a third neighbor pacing up and down his driveway, a worried look on his face.

"What's the matter with Ed?" one asked.

"He's worried about his son," the other answered.

"Why? What's he got?"

"The BMW!"

*

Junior came in the back door with a sad expression on his face. "What did your father say about the dent you put in the car?" his mother asked.

"Should I leave out all the swear words?"

"Please."

"Then he didn't say a thing."

*

Church Life

The little church was badly in need of repairs, so the pastor was making a fervent appeal for funds before the congregation. To everyone's surprise, the town miser stood up and pledged $100. As he sat back down in the stunned silence, a piece of plaster fell from above and landed on his head. "Guess I'd better make that two hundred," the miser announced.

From the back of the hall came a lone voice: "Hit him again, Lord!"

*

The evangelist was working up to the high point of his sermon. "There will be weeping, and wailing, and gnashing of teeth," he shouted.

Just then, an old woman stood up in the back. "Sir," she called, "I have no teeth."

"Madam," the evangelist replied, "teeth will be provided!"

*

A very old lady and a very small boy were seated together in the pew. As the collection plate approached, the little boy noticed the lady searching through her purse with an alarmed expression. Leaning over, he whispered, "Here, take my dime. I can hide under the seat."

*

A tiny boy of four was warned by his older sister that he couldn't talk in church. "They won't let you say anything," she said.

"Who won't?" the boy asked.

"The hushers," she replied.

*

When the deacon went to New York on vacation, his pastor asked him to order a sign to be put over the door of the church at Christmas. On the last day of his trip, the deacon remembered he needed to order a sign, but forgot the message, so he sent a wire to the pastor, asking for the dimensions and message. The lady at Western Union nearly had a fit when the pastor's wire came in: "Unto us a child is born. Eight feet long, three feet wide."

*

From a church bulletin: "Ushers will swat latecomers at these points in the service."

*

One Sunday a cowboy went to church. When he entered, he saw that he and the preacher were the only ones present. The preacher asked the cowboy if he wanted him to go ahead and preach. The cowboy said, "I'm not too smart, but if I went to feed my cattle and only one showed up, I'd feed him." So the minister began his sermon.

One hour passed, then two hours, then two-and-a-half hours. The preacher finally finished and came down to ask the cowboy how he had liked the sermon. The cowboy answered slowly, "Well, I'm not very smart, but if I went to feed my cattle and only one showed up, I sure wouldn't feed him *all* the hay."

*

Two clerics were visiting New York City on church business. The first, who tended to think more like a monk than the second, picked up the menu, saw the high cost of a New York meal, and intoned, "Now is a good time to put a bridle on our appetites."

The second just shrugged. "No, I think this is a good time to put a bit in our mouths."

*

The minister was good and worked up by his sermon on the duty of wives to be submissive to their husbands. "I see in our congregation today a woman who has disobeyed her husband," he said, picking up his hymnal. "To point her out to you all, I will now throw this book at her head."

Before he even got his arm over his head, *all* the women in the congregation had ducked.

*

The young seminarian was filling in for the church's minister, a very popular preacher who had suddenly been taken ill. Although he was obviously nervous, the youth gave a respectable sermon, then concluded his prayers with a fervent, "And may Pastor Hale be filled full of fresh veal and new zigor!"

*

The parishioner had asked the pastor to pray for him the following Sunday, but the pastor was reluctant. "Joe, I understand this is a serious problem, but we usually don't pray about floating kidneys during the service."

"It's not that much different from the other sick people you prayed for last Sunday, pastor."

"Which sick people?"

"All the ones with loose livers!"

*

The Sunday school teacher asked her class, "Does anyone know who lived in the Garden of Eden?"

"I do, teacher," said little Mary. "It was the Adams Family."

*

Just as the preacher was about to enter the pulpit, a woman in the congregation handed him a note requesting the congregation's prayers for her husband. The note read: "Bill Adams having gone to sea, his wife desires the congregation's prayers for his safety."

But the preacher was pressed for time and read the note a little too hastily, telling the congregation that, "Bill Adams, having gone to see his wife, desires the prayers of the congregation for his safety."

*

Even without TV and special effects, some old-time traveling preachers still managed to be quite theatrical. One of them would hire a young boy to climb into the rafters and hide there with a caged dove. At the climax of his appeal, the preacher would raise his hands, look toward heaven, and call, "Holy Ghost, come down!" The boy would release the dove on cue and it would fly down with great effect.

But one day when the preacher called, "Holy Ghost, come down!" nothing happened. He tried again, a little louder, "Holy Ghost, come down!"

Scuffling sounds were heard from the rafters, followed by a little voice that said, "Preacher, a big yellow cat just ate the Holy Ghost. You want me to throw down the yellow cat?"

*

The atheist was doing everything in his power to disrupt the evangelist's tent meeting — snickering, talking to his friends, asking irrelevant questions — and the evangelist was rapidly running out of patience. "Do you really believe that Jonah was swallowed by a whale?" the atheist called out sarcastically.

"When I get to heaven, I'll ask Jonah," the evangelist answered with a sigh.

"What if he's not there?"

"Then you'll just have to ask him, won't you?" snapped the evangelist.

*

Country

A car with two city men in it worked its way down the country road and passed a tumbledown shack with a stubble-faced farmer on the front porch. It had been a dull day and the driver felt he could use just a little fun, so he stopped the car and said, "Hey, mister, can you change an eighteen-dollar bill?"

The farmer nodded. "Sure thing, but I have to go inside to get the money." With that, he disappeared inside.

The driver's companion said, "What are you planning to do?"

"I'm giving him a ten," snickered the driver. "I'll mark up the zero to look like an eight. He'll never know the difference."

The farmer reappeared with a battered wallet. He took the bill offered him with the barest glance and put it into his pocket. Then he looked up and said, "How do you want the change? Two nines or three sixes?"

-Isaac Asimov

*

The New York artist was talking to a Vermont farmer who had a house to sell. "The house I buy must have a wonderful view, because I'm an artist. Does your house have a view?"

"Well," allowed the farmer, "from the porch you can see Joe Ludlow's barn. But beyond that, there's nothing but a bunch of mountains."

*

A small town is where you can finish your Sunday paper at breakfast.

*

A New York couple, lured by an ad, booked a room for a vacation at a Vermont hotel, but didn't like what they saw when they got there. "Why, you have more cows than you do guests," expostulated the man. "How do you explain that?"

Snapped the Vermonter, "We prefer 'em."

-Bennett Cerf

*

From a rural district of England comes the story of a driver of a small sedan braking hastily as the tweedy mistress of the largest estate thereabouts came hurtling around a sharp bend in the narrow road in her large Rolls. Before he could say a word, she shouted "PIG!" and drove on.

"Fat old cow!" he cried after her in retaliation. Then he drove around the bend himself — and crashed head-on into the biggest pig he'd ever seen.

-Bennett Cerf

*

The old farmer sat rocking on the front porch as he talked to the stranger. "Been thirty years since I lost my wife in those woods."

"Oh, I'm sorry. It must be hard to lose your wife like that."

"Hard?" the farmer snorted. "Was darn near impossible. She knew those woods like the back of her hand!"

*

"Did you hear about the farmer's daughter? She was so ugly that when she stood in the cornfield, the crows thought she was a scarecrow."

"Did she scare the crows away?"

"She scared them so much they brought back the corn they'd taken three days ago!"

*

25

"What a lovely area," the tourist gushed to the general-store clerk. "The mountains, the rivers, the wild animals. Tell me, have you lived here all your life?"

"Not yet," the clerk replied.

*

The old farmer finally decided it was time to buy some life insurance, but since he was in his seventies, he had to take a rigorous physical.

"Ever have any serious illnesses?" the doctor asked.

"Nope."

"What about accidents?"

"Nope."

"Wait. You mean you've never had an accident in your life?"

"Nope."

"Didn't I see you in Doc Jacob's getting your leg set last year?"

"Yup."

"What happened to it?"

"Bull tossed me over the fence."

"Well, that was an accident, wasn't it?"

"Nope. He did it on purpose!"

*

The old farmer and his wife were enjoying their first day in town in months, looking in every store window, reading every sign. But when they got to the plumbing store, he just shook his head at the sign in the window: **Cast Iron Sinks.**

"Martha," he said to his wife, "people in town must be getting stupid. Who doesn't know that cast iron sinks?"

*

The farmer was driving by the insane asylum when an inmate yelled out to him, "What's in your truck?"

"Manure," the farmer called back.

"What are you going to do with it?"

"Put it on my strawberries."

"Hah! I may be crazy, but at least I know enough to use sugar and cream!"

*

"Had trouble with both my wives," the farmer admitted.

"What kind of trouble?"

"First one ran off on me."

"Oh, I'm sorry. And the second?"

"Didn't."

*

"Had to shoot my dog the other day," said Eb.

"Was he mad?"

"Weren't too pleased."

*

The two farmers had looked at each other at the post office every day for the last twenty years, nodded, then gone on their way. One day one of them turned left instead of right on leaving the post office and the other caled out, "Lew! Where you going?"

"None of your business!" Lew snapped. "And I wouldn't tell you that much if we wasn't such close friends."

*

The tourist made a mad dash down the dock, gathered himself up, and dove over five feet of water to land on the deck of the ferry. "I made it!" he announced proudly.

"Yup," said the deckhand. "But this boat is on the way *in*."

*

The circulation office of the local paper sent a note to Joe Parish, saying his subscription had expired. The note came back with this scrawled on top of it: "So's Joe."

*

The backwoodsman finally came into town and decided to see his very first movie, a western. He seemed particularly interested in the scene where the women from the wagon train went bathing in a pond. The scene was done in good taste, though, since a passing train blotted out the view of the pond just as the women began to leave the water.

Late that evening, an usher approached the backwoodsman and whispered, "Sir, you've seen this movie three times. How long are you planning to stay?"

"Well," the man replied, "I figure on leaving soon. That train'll be off-schedule sooner or later."

*

Two fellows had been hunting all day with no luck when a huge bear suddenly appeared over a hill, caught their scent, and began lumbering in their direction. One of the men immediately reached into his pack, pulled out a pair of sneakers, and began lacing them up as fast as he could. His friend said to him, "You know you can't outrun that bear, don't you?"

"Don't have to outrun that bear," the other replied. "Only have to outrun you!"

*

Doctors and Dentists

Tom Parker tells about a colleague who tried to steal patients from the medico who shared his office with him and was promptly sued for alienation of infections.

-Bennett Cerf

*

"I had the strangest dream last night," the patient confided to his analyst. "I dreamed that you were my mother!"

"Your mother?" echoed the analyst, his interest instantly aroused. "I wonder what provoked a dream like that? Tell me the details."

"Well," said the patient, "I dreamed that I woke up at my regular hour in the morning and came to you for my regular breakfast of three hamburgers and an ice cream soda."

"Ridiculous," interrupted the analyst. "What kind of a breakfast is that for a healthy young man?"

-Bennett Cerf

*

A *farbissener* doctor was called to the hut of a shoemaker whose wife was seriously ill.

"Please, doctor. Save her!" cried the husband. "I'll pay anything, even if I have to sell everything I own."

"But what if I can't cure her?" said the doctor shrewdly.

"I'll pay you whether you cure her or kill her!" cried the desperate husband.

A week later, the woman died. The doctor sent the shoemaker a huge bill. And now the poor man suggested they both go to the rabbi to discuss the fee.

29

The rabbi, who knew the doctor's reputation, said, "What was your agreement with this man?"

"He agreed to pay me for treating his wife," said the doctor, "whether I cured her or killed her."

"And did you cure her?"

"No."

"Did you kill her?"

"Certainly not!"

"Then," said the rabbi, "under what contract are you claiming your fee?"

-Leo Rosten

*

Two old men were arguing the merits of their respective doctors. The first one said, "I don't trust your fancy doctor. He treated old Jake Waxman for a kidney ailment for nearly a year, and then Jake died of a liver ailment."

"So what makes you think your doctor is any better?" asked his friend.

"Because when my doctor treats you for a kidney ailment, you can be sure you'll *die* of a kidney ailment."

-George Jessel

*

Two colleagues were discussing a patient. "I was having great success with Mr. Green," said the first doctor. "When he first came to me, he was suffering from a massive inferiority complex related to his size."

"How did you treat this patient?" asked the second doctor.

"I started out with intensive analysis and then group therapy. I convinced him that many of the world's greatest leaders were men of small physical stature. I really hated to lose Mr. Green."

"What do you mean? How did you lose him?"

"Terrible accident," replied the physician. " A pussycat ate him."

-George Jessel

*

My doctor just drops a note to his fully recovered patients: "Just pay me half of what you offered to pay me when you thought you were dying."

-Sam Levenson

*

A national research company compiled a mailing list from doctors' active files and sent this question to 10,000 patients: Do you trust your doctor? Sixty percent replied yes. Twenty percent replied "Only when I'm feeling well." Twenty percent came back marked "Deceased."

-Sam Levenson

*

So this druggist is filling a prescription, hands his customer a little bottle with twelve pills in it, and says, "That'll be four-fifty." Suddenly the phone rings, and as the druggist turns to answer it, the customer puts fifty cents on the counter and walks out. The druggist turns, spots the fifty cents, and yells, "Sir! Sir! That's four-fifty, not fifty cents." The guy is gone. The druggist picks up the half a buck, shrugs, flips it into the till, and mumbles, "Oh well, a forty-cent profit is better than nothing."

-Robert Orben

*

A psychiatrist was sitting on a park bench, his head in his hands, weeping softly to himself. A colleague walking by noticed and decided to lend a sympathetic ear. "What's depressed you so? You have a thriving practice and a wonderful family life."

"You know that man who thought he was Captain Kirk? The one I had committed to the state mental hospital last year?"

"The one you wrote the papers on?"

"That's the one. He escaped last night. Just as I was starting to make real progress in convincing him that he wasn't a time-traveling Star Fleet commander."

"Gee, that's a shame. How'd he get away from the hospital?"

"Scotty beamed him up."

*

The dentist picked up the office phone and nodded sympathetically as one of his patients described a problem he was having. "Hm. yes. Well, come in tomorrow morning and I'll have a look. Today? No, I'm sorry, but I have eighteen cavities to fill today. See you tomorrow at nine." Dutifully noting the appointment on his calendar, he then picked up his golf bag and left the office whistling.

*

"How long has your wife believed she's a chicken?" the psychiatrist asked the husband.

"Three years, doc."

"Three years! Why did you wait so long before bringing her to see me?"

"Well, we really needed the eggs."

*

"You're as normal as I am, Mr. Toon," the psychiatrist said.

"But what about all these butterflies? They're all over me!" the patient cried as he brushed the front of his shirt.

"For heaven's sake," yelled the doctor, "don't get them all on me!"

*

Whistler, of *Whistler's Mother* fame, was not noted for his social graces, so when his beloved dog developed a throat problem, he had no qualms about calling in a famous throat surgeon. The surgeon looked at the dog, prescribed some medicine, charged Whistler a healthy fee, and went on his way — fuming.

The next day, the surgeon left a message that he needed to see Whistler as soon as possible. Whistler, assuming the doctor wanted to talk about his dog, dropped everything and rushed to the doctor's office. The doctor met the artist at the front door. "Thank you for coming right over, Mr. Whistler," he said. "I wanted to see you about having this door painted."

*

The struggling young pediatrician put the following sign up beside his office door: "Small fevers gratefully received."

*

Family

Soon after the election of 1912, Woodrow Wilson visited a beloved aunt who was hard of hearing. She asked Wilson how he was making a living now, so he told her, in a loud voice, that he was the president.

"Of what?" his aunt inquired.

"Of the country," Wilson shouted back.

"Don't be silly!" the old lady replied with a snort.

*

Misers may not be much fun to live with, but they sure do make great ancestors!

*

Three fathers at a church meeting were talking about what they would do if a burglar broke into their houses at night.

"I'd call the police," said the first.

"I'd have my wife call the police while I grabbed the baseball bat," growled the second.

The third man, the father of three preschoolers, admitted, "If a burglar came into my room at night, I'd probably get up and take him to the bathroom."

*

My son is getting out of college, and not a dollar too soon! He's already finished four years and a bank account. Last month he wrote me a letter: "Dear Pop: Haven't heard from you in weeks. Send me a check so I'll know you're all right!"

-Robert Orben

The ladies met on the Grand Concourse, Mrs. Blumenfeld carrying her groceries, Mrs. Kovarsky pushing a pram with two little boys in it.

"Good morning, Mrs. Kovarsky. Such darling little boys! So how old are they?"

"The doctor," said Mrs. Kovarsky, "is three, and the lawyer is two."

-Leo Rosten

*

Mrs. Siegel confided to her neighbor that her son had gone through so miserable a phase that he was now seeing a psychoanalyst. "And the doctor says my Marvin is suffering from an Oedipus complex!"

"Oedipus-Shmoedipus," scoffed her neighbor. "So long as he loves his mother."

-Leo Rosten

*

"Will you please stand as I call your names?" our school principal asked the mothers at the PTA tea. "I'm sure the teachers would like to tie you up with your children."

*

Doctors will tell you that if you eat slowly you will eat less. Anyone raised in a large family will tell you the same thing.

-Sam Levenson

*

When Mr. Bauman had to go to London on business, he persuaded his brother to take care of his Siamese cat while he was away. Mr. Bauman dearly loved that Siamese cat, but the brother definitely did not. The very moment Bauman set foot back at Kennedy Airport, he phoned his brother to check on the cat's health. The brother announced curtly, "Your cat died," and hung up. Mr. Bauman was inconsolable. Finally, however, he phoned his brother again to point out, "It was needlessly cruel and sadistic of you to tell me that bluntly that my poor cat had passed away."

"What did you expect me to do?" demanded the brother.

"You could have broken the bad news gradually," grumbled Bauman." First, you could have said the cat was playing on the roof. Later you could have called to say he fell off. The next morning, you could have reported he had broken his leg. Then, when I came to get him, you could have told me he had passed away during the night. Well — you didn't have it in you to be that civilized. Now tell me — how's Mom?"

The brother pondered momentarily, then announced, "She's playing on the roof."

-Bennett Cerf

*

Old Lady Abernathy hadn't seen her young grandson since his christening, and when she heard he was being sent up to her country place to spend his ninth birthday with her, she was so delighted she put five dollars in the collection plate that Sunday at church.

The Sunday after her grandson went back home, she put in ten dollars.

-Bennett Cerf

*

A harassed housewife tells about the crook who broke into her car and took thirty-five dollars worth of groceries—out of her glove compartment.

*

I understand the only people in the world who have no juvenile delinquency problem are the Eskimos — and it's all because of whale blubber. The minute a kid steps out of line, they whale him till he blubbers.

-Robert Orben

*

During the Gold Rush, when thousands of men lived for years without their families, a young mother took her infant to the theater one evening. Just as the orchestra began to play, the baby broke into loud wails.

"Stop those fiddles and let the baby cry," called a man from the audience. "I haven't heard that sound in ten years!"

The audience heartily applauded his sentiment, the music was stopped, and the lonely prospectors happily sat and listened to the crying baby.

*

What do you call a man with one car, a wife, and three teenagers? A pedestrian.

*

"Dad," the boy asked his father, "what's a necessary evil?"

"A necessary evil is one we like so much we don't want to abolish it, son."

*

What's the punishment for bigamy? Two mothers-in-law!

-Michael Johnstone

*

What's the difference between a misfortune and a calamity? If your mother-in-law drives into the river, that's a misfortune. If she was driving your BMW, that's a calamity.

Friends and Neighbors

Things never were the same at Robert and Betty Thumma's farm after their silo caught fire. They called the fire department, but the firefighters just couldn't get it out. The fire seemed to go out, but it smoldered and burst into flame several times. The chief decided the best thing to do was just let it burn itself out, which it did for at least three weeks.

And that's when people driving past the farm started stopping to tell the Thummas that their silo was on fire. It happened all day and all night. Finally, the Thummas decided to put up a large sign at the side of the road near the silo:

Yes, we know the silo's burning. Thanks.

-John Bohannon

*

Mark Twain, a man who enjoyed dressing comfortably if not properly, often visited friends without his collar and tie. One day his wife caught him returning from a neighbor's without his collar and tie and scolded him roundly for it. Twain went to his room, dug out a collar and tie, wrapped them up, and had them sent to his neighbor with the following note: "A little while ago I visited you without my collar and tie. The missing articles are enclosed. Will you kindly gaze at them for thirty minutes and then return them to me?"

*

Harry leaned over the back fence to speak an encouraging word to his sick neighbor. "What'd the doctor say yesterday, Pete?"

"He said I only have a month to live," Pete answered with a smile.

"That's terrible! How can you smile about that?"

"I'm not stupid, Harry. After I left him, I went to eleven other doctors and got a month from each of them, so now I have a whole year. That's not bad for someone as sick as I am!"

*

Government

A few years ago, when the U.S. Ping-Pong team was returning from Hong Kong after a successful tour overseas, Senators Hiram Fong of Hawaii and William Spong of Virginia asked that bells be played in Honolulu when the team came home. They introduced a bill for this in the Congress, and it became known as the Spong-Fong Ping-Pong Hong Kong Dingdong Bell Bill.

-John Bohannon

*

The U.S. Postal Service had occupied a building in suburban Dallas for thirty years when the building was sold. The new landlord raised the rent, but postal officials objected and withheld payment. The landlord sued them, and they decided to pay up. But the check failed to reach the landlord on time, and a federal judge signed an eviction notice.

The check had been delayed in the mail.

*

The U.S. Department of Agriculture recently issued a booklet titled, "What to Do With Your Fertilizer During an Enemy Attack."

-John Bohannon

*

You know what the Pentagon is. That's a big building in Washington that has five sides—on almost every issue.

-Robert Orben

*

Sign in a service station: We collect taxes—federal, state, and local. We also sell gasoline as a sideline.

*

An American is not afraid to tell off the President of the United States; but he's always polite to a meter maid.

-Sam Levenson

*

If you can keep your head when all about you are losing theirs, maybe you haven't heard the news.

*

Politics is the art of looking for trouble, finding it everywhere, diagnosing it incorrectly, and applying the wrong remedies.

*

Only one man in a million understands the international situation. Isn't it odd how you keep running into him at parties?

*

The hardest job Congress has is getting money from the taxpayers without disturbing the voters.

*

The mail service has obviously seen better days, but once upon a time, it must have been impressive. Some of Mark Twain's friends decided to send him a letter congratulating him on his birthday, but none of them knew exactly where he was, since Twain toured and spoke all over the world. Taking a shot anyway, they simply addressed their letter to: "Mark Twain. God knows where."

Several weeks later they received a short reply from Twain: "He did."

*

Kreiger needed a brain transplant, so he went down to the organ bank to pick one out.

"This one belonged to a philosopher," the manager said. "It costs five thousand dollars. If that doesn't suit you, here's one donated by a nuclear physicist. It's eight thousand. And that one over there was taken from a politician. It's one hundred thousand dollars."

"Wait a minute. If a philosopher's brain goes for five thousand and a scientist's for eight, how come a politician's costs one hundred thousand?"

"Because it's never been used, of course!"

*

"I've got good news and bad news, Mr. Philby," the IRS examiner said. "The bad news is, we still aren't through with your audit. The good news is, we've seen enough to be sure you can sell the fiction rights at a great price."

*

We're having so much trouble overseas that the government's developed a prefab embassy building. It comes with the windows already broken out.

*

Three men in Detroit know how to cut the defense budget, if someone would only ask them: You use last year's rockets. You just redesign the fins a little.

*

Scientists and postal workers control the world. The scientists smash the atom; the post office smashes everything else.

*

My mother sent a Bible to my son by parcel post. When it got here, seven of the Ten Commandments were already broken.

*

The Japanese are bringing in a new car this year. It's called a Congress: It sounds great, but can't pass anything.

*

It may be true that the only sure things in life are death and taxes, but at least death doesn't get worse every time Congress meets!

*

Groaners

What's brown and sneaks around the kitchen at Thanksgiving? Mince spies.

-Michael Johnstone

*

What did the grape say when the elephant stepped on it? Nothing. It just gave out a little whine.

-Michael Johnstone

*

Where did Noah keep his bees? In the archives.

*

Name the world's only surviving kamikaze pilot. Chicken Teriyaki.

*

Why do elephants paint their toenails red, green, orange, black, and purple? So they can hide in the jelly bean jar.

*

There's nothing unsafe about the streets of New York. It's the people on top of them you have to watch out for.

*

Why did the elephant sit on the marshmallow? So he wouldn't burn his toes in the hot cocoa.

*

Where does the Lone Ranger take his garbage? To the dump, to the dump, to the dump, dump, dump.

*

What did the space visitor say to the gas pump? Take your finger out of your ear and listen to me!

*

What did they tell the cannibal who came to dinner late? Everybody's eaten.

*

What's green, noisy, and extremely dangerous? A herd of stampeding pickles.

*

"I'm afraid you have canary fever," the doctor said to his patient.
"Canary fever? Is that serious?"
"Yes," the doctor admitted. "But it's tweetable."

*

History

Frederick II, the eighteenth-century king of Prussia, fancied himself an enlightened monarch, and in some respects he was. On one occasion he is supposed to have interested himself in conditions in the Berlin prison and was escorted through it so that he might speak to the prisoners. One after the other, the prisoners fell to their knees before him, bewailing their lot and, predictably, protesting their utter innocence of all charges that had been brought against them.

Only one prisoner remained silent, and finally Frederick's curiosity was aroused. "You," he called. "You there."

The prisoner looked up. "Yes, Your Majesty?"

"Why are you here?"

"Armed robbery, Your Majesty."

"And are you guilty?"

"Entirely guilty, Your Majesty. I richly deserve my punishment."

At this, Frederick rapped his cane sharply on the ground and said, "Warden, release this guilty wretch at once. I will not have him here in jail, where by example he will corrupt all the splendid, innocent people who occupy it!"

-Isaac Asimov

*

When he was in college, Calvin Coolidge boarded at the cheapest house he could find, which was probably why hash appeared on the menu so often. Each time it did, Coolidge went through the same routine. "Where is the dog?" he would ask. The dog would be called in. "And the cat?" The cat would be brought in. Then, and only then, would Coolidge eat his hash!

*

It is said that a hostile voter once accosted Churchill immediately after an election in which the latter had retained his seat in Parliament. The voter said with a sneer, "I presume we may expect you to continue to be humbly subservient to the powerful interests that control your vote."

To which Churchill replied with a growl, "I'll thank you to keep my wife out of this."

-Isaac Asimov

*

Franklin D. Roosevelt, when told that Wendell Wilkie had his eye on the presidential chair, is said to have answered, "Yes, but look what *I've* got on it."

-Bennett Cerf

*

Cordell Hull, the American secretary of state from 1933 to 1944, was reputed to be an extremely cautious man ungiven to advancing an opinion past the evidence, as perhaps befits a secretary of state. Once, on a train trip, Hull and a companion watched while the train dragged its load of cars slowly past a large flock of sheep.

Making conversation, Hull's companion said, "Those sheep have recently been sheared."

Hull stared thoughtfully at the animals, then said, "Appears so. At least on the side facing us."

-Isaac Asimov

*

At a government function in the nineteen-twenties, a young lady took the privilage of her sex and, approaching President Coolidge said gushingly, "Oh, Mr. President, I have made a wager with a friend of mine that I could persuade you to say more than two words to me. Could you?"

Coolidge, without expression, said, "You lose."

-Isaac Asimov

*

Thomas Edison had been staying up late for several weeks working on the electric light bulb. In principle, it was simple, but finding the right material for the filament proved daunting. One night, in the wee small hours, he finally discovered just the substance he needed and built the first light bulb. To his delight, it lit and burned steadily. Overjoyed, he picked the whole thing up and charged into his room, where his wife was fast asleep.

"Darling, look! Look what I've invented!"

Mrs. Edison rolled over and said, "For heaven's sake, Tom, turn out the light and come to bed!"

*

Daniel Webster was once sued by his butcher for not paying his bill. Before the matter went to court, Webster met the butcher on the street and asked why the man hadn't sent for Webster's meat order.

"I didn't think you'd want to deal with me once I brought suit against you," the butcher replied.

"Sue all you wish," Webster said, "but don't try to starve me to death!"

*

As you can imagine, the real Noah Webster was a stickler about the correct usage of words. One day his wife wandered into their garden and found Noah kissing the maid.

"I'm surprised!" Mrs Webster exclaimed.

"No, dear," Noah corrected. "You are astonished. We are surprised."

*

Cecil Rhodes was once asked why he had left England to settle in Africa. Was it because of his health or because of his love of adventure?

"The truth is," Rhodes admitted, "I could no longer stand England's eternal cold mutton!"

*

Mark Twain's vocabulary contained a good number of swear words that he used regularly, despite the protests of his wife. One day after Twain had used them all while cutting himself shaving, Mrs. Twain accurately repeated every swear word, just to show Twain how terrible he sounded. Twain calmly told her, "You have the words, dear, but you don't know the tune."

*

It's said that Noel Coward once sent the same note to twenty of the most influential men in London: "All is discovered. Escape while you can." All twenty left town before the end of the day.

*

Violinist Fritz Kreisler and a friend, out walking one day, happened to pass a fish store. In the window was a huge display of fresh fish arranged in a row, their mouths gaping open and their eyes staring blankly ahead.

"Good heavens!" Kreisler exclaimed. "That reminds me — I'm late for a concert!"

Holidays

Here it is the middle of January and we're still cleaning up from Christmas. Last week we cleaned out our checking account; this week we cleaned out our savings account.

-Robert Orben

*

I'm beginning to wonder if it was a good idea to give the six-year-old one of those rockets that actually blast off. As of this morning, we've got the only cat in the neighborhood who knows what our house looks like from 300 feet up!

-Robert Orben

*

If you're planning a vacation in Atlantic City, you're going to a remarkable place. Where else can you drive into town in a $10,000 car and leave in a $100,000 bus?

*

Did you hear about Frank Purdue's new line for conservatives? Turkeys with two right wings.

*

Disarmament doesn't stand a chance. Oh, we're all for it. So are the Russians. But the toy manufacturers?

*

I gave my building super the same thing for Christmas that he gave me all year— absolutely nothing.

*

With all the terrorism around Europe, wouldn't it make more sense to bring home our Marines over there and just arm our tourists?

*

You think men don't fool around on cruises? The last time they played "O Come, All Ye Faithful" on a holiday cruise, only three men showed up.

*

You want to get a lot of Christmas cards this year? Around Thanksgiving, tell everyone about the chalet you just bought in Aspen.

*

Humor

The English are notoriously slow in getting a joke. In a way, it's very economical, because you get three laughs everytime you tell an Englishman a joke. He laughs when you tell it, to be polite. Two hours later, he laughs again, when he gets it. And the next day he laughs a third time, when he finally understands it.

*

That's why they don't show comedies on English television Saturday nights. All the unexpected laughter disrupts Sunday's sermon.

*

On the other hand, an American never really laughs at any joke. He's heard them all before, and an American doesn't need to be polite to anyone.

*

"I heard a great joke the other day. Did I tell it to you?"
"Was it funny?"
"It was hysterical!"
"Then you didn't."

*

Husbands and Wives

An eccentric millionaire once sent a henchman around the countryside. He was to interview the householders, and to every man who was boss in his house, he was to give a horse. To every man who was henpecked, he would give a chicken.

Everywhere the henchman went, he handed out chickens, with never an occasion to once give anyone a horse. At last, though, he arrived at the house of a burly farmer with a bristly, unshaven face, a deep bass voice, and muscles like an ox. In the background was his thin and wizened wife.

The henchman said, "Are you the boss in your family, sir?"

The farmer leaned his head back and bellowed with laughter. "You bet, little man," he said. "What I say around here goes!" And he opened and closed fists the size of hams.

The henchman was convinced. "You get a horse," he said. "Do you want a brown horse or a gray horse?"

The farmer reared his head back and shouted, "Tilda, do we get a brown horse or a gray horse?"

Tilda called back, "You get a brown horse."

And the henchman said, "You get a chicken."

-Isaac Asimov

*

The husband had half listened to his wife as she gossiped on the telephone for what seemed, to him, far too long. Understanding the nature of gossip, he rebuked her mildly when she finally hung up: "Dear, I think you stretch the truth a little sometimes."

"Really?" she replied. "I thought it was a wife's duty to say nice things about her husband now and then."

*

"How do you like married life, Joe?"
"Well, she does treat me like a god."
"That's great! What's she do?"
"Places a burnt offering before me every night."

*

When the prospector's wife asked him to name his new mine after he, he cheerfully agreed. That's why one of the richest gold mines in the country is known as the Holy Terror.

*

A famous woman author was registering alone at a swank hotel while on tour promoting her latest book. The desk clerk asked her occupation. "Author," the woman replied.

"Housewife," the clerk muttered to himself.

"Author," repeated the writer.

"I'll just put down housewife," the clerk insisted. "And what's your husband's profession?"

"Why don't you just put down housewife?" the irritated author snapped.

*

Man can climb the highest mountain, swim the widest ocean, fight the strongest tiger, but once he's married, mostly he takes out the garbage.

-Sam Levenson

*

All I want is the right to sit at the steering wheel in the family car in front of the house at seven A.M. and honk the horn continuously for a half hour while my husband dresses the children for school.

-Sam Levenson

*

My husband was just named by his college as Man of the Year; which shows you what kind of year this has been.

-Sam Levenson

*

Asked to tell his class something about the Quakers, the little boy replied, "The Quakers are very meek, quiet people who never fight or answer back. I think my father is a Quaker. Not my mother."

-Sam Levenson

*

A pompous old windbag put a nickel into one of those weighing machines that tell your fortune as a bonus. He proudly read the card he got aloud to his wife. It said:" You are brilliant, witty, and irresistible to the opposite sex."

His wife nodded grimly and snapped, "It's got your weight wrong, too!"

-Bennett Cerf

*

"My life has not been an easy one," the man told his new acquaintance. "I've been widowed three times. The first two wives died of eating poisoned mushrooms. The third, poor thing, passed away as the result of a concussion."

"A concussion, you say?" murmured the new acquaintance. " How did that happen?"

"A very sad case, " sighed the widower. "I couldn't get her to eat the mushrooms."

-Bennett Cerf

*

The pastor mumbles a few words in church and you're married. A few months later, you mumble a few words in your sleep and you're divorced.

*

Sweet young thing to her lawyer: "If I take out a million-dollar insurance policy on my husband today and he dies tomorrow, what would I get?"

"Life."

*

"Dad, did Edison invent the talking machine?"

"No, son. God did that. But Edison invented the first one that could be turned off."

*

The eighty-year-old woman stood before the judge, asking for a divorce from her eighty-two-year-old husband.

"How long have you two been married?" the judge inquired.

"Sixty years."

"Sixty years? Why do you want a divorce after sixty years of marriage?"

"Enough is enough."

*

Before we were married, my wife always told me, "You're only interested in one thing!" Wish I could remember what she was talking about!

*

"There goes my wife, the human dynamo."

"She's a dynamo?"

"Sure is. Everything on her is charged."

*

"Dad," the little boy asked, "is it true that married men live longer than single men?"

"No, son. It just seems longer."

*

The old man struggled onto his knees in front of the luscious twenty-year-old. "My dear," he wheezed, "I have five million dollars, but I'm eighty years old. Will you marry me? Or am I too old?"

"Too old?" she replied. "Darling, I'd be perfectly happy if you were ten years older!"

*

Why do women live longer than men? Because paint's a great preservative.

*

What'd the cannibal's wife say when he brought home an actor? "Oh, good! Ham sandwiches!"

*

The husband drove down to the police station and said to the officer at the desk, " I'm Jake Nelson. Could I talk to the guy you arrested for robbing our house last night"

"What for?"

"I'd really love to know how he got into the house without waking up my wife."

*

"Is your wife outspoken?"

"Not by anyone I've ever met."

*

The policeman said to the husband, "The neighbors say you and your wife have had some words."

"Humpf!" the husband snorted. "I had some, but I never got a chance to use them!"

*

The wife had been talking for at least ten minutes before she looked over to where her husband was sitting, absorbed in the newspaper. "Why don't you answer me?" she demanded.

"I did," he replied, turning a page.

"No, you didn't."

"I shook my head no."

"Oh, pardon me. I guess I didn't hear the rattle."

*

Knock Knocks

Knock knock.
Who's there?
Mandy.
Mandy who?
Mandy torpedoes, full speed ahead.

*

Knock knock.
Who's there?
Diesel.
Diesel who?
Diesel make you laugh.

*

Knock knock.
Who's there?
Dishes.
Dishes who?
Dishes the police. Open the door.

*

Knock knock.
Who's there?
Little old lady.
Little old lady who?
Gee, I didn't know you could yodel!

*

Knock knock.
Who's there?
Fire engine.
Fire engine who?
Fire engine one, we're blasting off.

*

The Law

The young lawyer had tried the judge's patience all through the trial, objecting to every decision and making the courtroom into his own personal stage, but at last it was over. "I sentence you to one year in jail and a seventy-five-dollar fine," the judge said.

The young lawyer immediately jumped to his feet and called out, "I'm going to fight to have the sentence reversed."

"Certainly," said the judge, with a smile that churned the stomach of everyone there who knew him. "Perhaps you'd prefer seventy-five years in jail and a one-dollar fine?"

*

The judge was questioning the witness about a shot that had allegedly been fired. "Did you *see* the shot fired?" he asked her.

Temporarily flustered, the witness replied, "Well, no. But I *heard* it."

"That's not good enough," he ruled. "You're excused. "

As she left the box, the witness shrugged and laughed, setting the spectators and jury to giggling. The judge promptly fined her for contempt of court.

The witness hung her head for a moment, then asked softly, "Did you *see* me laugh, sir?"

"No, but I certainly heard you."

"That's not good enough, Your Honor," she replied. The fine was canceled.

*

The local police station received a call from a citizen reporting that he had been beaten up in the dark outside his own back door but hadn't seen his assailant.

The policeman sent out to investigate reported back after several minutes. "I solved the case," he reported.

"Good going," said the sergeant. "How did you do it?"

"*I* stepped on the rake, too," the officer admitted, touching the growing lump on his forehead.

*

Inscription on a headstone: *Here lies a lawyer and an honest man.*

A passerby remarked, "It's hard to believe there's room enough for two people in that grave."

*

An old Southerner was hauled into court for vagrancy. The judge asked his name.

"Colonel Ebenezer Jackson," the defendant responded.

"What does the 'Colonel' stand for?"

"Well, it's kinda like the 'Honorable' in front of your name. Doesn't mean a darn thing."

*

A man was charged with shooting a number of pigeons belonging to a farmer, and the counsel for the defense tried to intimidate the farmer during his cross-examination. "Are you prepared to swear that this man shot your pigeons?"

"I didn't say he shot them. I said I suspected him of doing it."

"Aha! What made you *suspect* my client?"

"First of all, I caught him on my land with a gun. Second, I heard a gun go off and saw some pigeons fall. Third, I found four of my pigeons in his pocket, and I don't think they flew in there and committed suicide!"

*

Sign in a police station: Thirty days hath September, April, June, and the speed offender.

*

The devil and St. Peter were having an argument over the wall that separates heaven from hell, which was crumbling in several places. St. Peter insisted that it was the devil's job to repair it. "If you don't repair this wall in one week, I'm going to sue you," snarled St. Peter.

"Oh, really? And where, may I ask, do you think you're going to find yourself a lawyer?"

-George Jessel

*

A lawyer, a doctor, and an architect are stranded on a desert island with no food, although across a shark-filled channel lies an island with lush coconut trees. The architect volunteers to swim across the channel for food, but as soon as he steps into the water, he's surrounded by sharks. When he jumps out, the doctor says he'll try to make it, but the same thing happens to him.

"Well, I guess it's up to me," says the lawyer, diving in. The sharks part for him and let him swim to the island, where he picks some coconuts. He dives back into the channel, the sharks once again give way, and he returns to the doctor and architect.

"Why did the sharks part for you?" asks the architect.

The lawyer shrugs and says, "Professional courtesy."

*

"Officer, you have to lock me up! I just hit my wife over the head with a club."

"That's terrible! Did you kill her?"

"Heavens, no. That's why you have to lock me up!"

*

"The defendant claims his wife was uncontrollable, Your Honor, so he beat her into submission with a golf club."

"How many strokes?"

*

"What were you and your wife fighting about?" the policeman asked the husband after he had quieted them both down.

"It was silly, really. She was trying to drive a nail into the wall with the back of her hairbrush. All I said was that that wouldn't work. Then she took after me like a madwoman with the hairbrush."

"That's all you said?"

"Well, I might have said something else."

"Like what?"

"I asked her why she didn't use her head."

*

I have a handshake deal with my lawyer. Every time I think of the deal, my hands shake!

*

A punctilious traffic court judge, having fined a speedster twenty-five dollars, suggested, "Better keep a receipt from the clerk when you pay up."

"What do you expect me to do with it?" snapped the disgruntled speedster.

"Save it," counseled his honor. "When you get three of them, you get a bicycle!"

-Bennett Cerf

*

The young lawyer had come to New York to try his first case, and he was scared silly by the time he reached the courtroom. Taking a deep breath, he tossed his coat onto a seat and stood before the judge.

"Young man, is the first time you've practiced in this city?" the judge asked sternly.

Afraid he had already done something terribly wrong, the lawyer admitted this was his first case in New York.

"In that case, go get your coat and put it where you can keep an eye on it," the judge advised.

*

The Chancellor of England, Lord Bacon, about to sentence a criminal, asked if he had anything to say.

"Yes, Your Honor. You should let me off, because we're related. My name is Hogg, and Hogg is kin to Bacon."

"Not," Lord Bacon replied, "until it's hung."

*

Lincoln would often go to great lengths to avoid unnecessary lawsuits. One day a man insisted on suing another man for $2.50, and nothing Lincoln said would convince him otherwise. So Lincoln agreed to represent the first man and asked for a $10 retainer. Once he had the money, Lincoln loaned $2.50 of it to the poor second man, who promptly repaid Lincoln's client and avoided the lawsuit.

*

One of the city's lawyers had died suddenly, leaving his widow without the funds to bury him, so all the city's lawyers took up a collection. When they called on the city judge for a donation, he replied, "A dollar? A dollar to bury a lawyer? Here's a twenty — bury twenty of them for me!"

*

The lawyer had to apologize to the judge or be held in contempt of court, so he rose and said, "Your Honor is right and I am wrong, as Your Honor generally is."

The judge accepted the apology with a puzzled look on his face.

*

Despite the fact that the day was sweltering, the judge was sipping hot coffee at the party. "Why don't you drink something that will cool you off?" his host asked him. "Have you ever tried gin and tonic?"

"No," replied the judge, "but I've tried many men who have."

Looks

"Why do you look so sad today, Joe?"
"My wife got hit by a truck yesterday."
"That's awful! You look pretty busted up."
"Yeah? Well, you should see my truck!"

*

Ever notice than men rarely have their faces lifted? That's because with a little patience, it'll grow right up through their hair.

*

"I always said I'd kill anyone I found who was uglier than me."
"Am I uglier than you?"
"Yes, you are."
"Please! Kill me!"

*

"Looks just like her mother, doesn't she?" asked the proud father.
"At least she's healthy."

*

The overweight woman stepped on the scale outside the drugstore. Two little boys nearby watched in astonishment as the needle moved up to seventy-five pounds and stopped dead. Since the machine was broken, everyone in town weighed seventy-five pounds, but the boys didn't know that. Finally one boy turned to the other and whispered, "She's hollow!"

*

Manners

A nine-year-old won his first literary prize for a school composition on manners. "I have good manners," he wrote. "I say good night and good morning and hello and good-bye, and when I see dead things lying around the house I bury them."

*

One day Lady Randolph invited George Bernard Shaw, the curmudgeonly writer, to lunch with her. He fired back a note saying, "Certainly not! What have I done to provoke such an attack on my well-known habits?"

Lady Randolph replied, "I know nothing of your habits. Hope they are not as bad as your manners."

*

The young society mother had invited a famous banker to tea and was reminding her young daughter how she should behave when she came in to be introduced. "Mr. Hill has a very large nose, dear, so be careful not to mention it. Don't even look at his nose. Just say hello politely, answer any of his questions, and then go back outside to play."

When the time came for her daughter to be introduced, the mother was relieved to have everything go smoothly; no mention was made of the banker's nose. Taking a deep breath in relief, she poured him some tea and inquired, "Now, Mr. Hill, will you have cream or lemon in your nose?"

*

As the intermission ended, a man leaned down and asked the occupant of the aisle seat, "Excuse me, but did someone step on your foot when the intermission began?"

"Yes, they did!"

"Okay, Martha," the questioner said, motioning to his wife. "This is our row."

*

Modern Life

The new father bought his son a five-hundred dollar bond. "That should just about be enough to allow him to treat us to a dinner on the day he graduates from college," he said to his wife.

*

I hear the big food companies are working on a tearless onion, and I think they can do it. They've already given us tasteless bread.

-Robert Orben

*

Man often fails to meet the strain put upon him by his own inventions: "I'd pay my utility bill right away but I can't tell the meter number from the estimated consumption number, the account number, the computer code number, the last date of inspection number, the credit due number, or the threatened date of shut-off number."

-Sam Levenson

*

The scientists have given us bombs and detergents so powerful we don't know whether we are going to be blown to bits or foamed to death.

-Sam Levenson

*

Habitual dependence on automation can lead to atrophy of the brain. Incredible as it seems, this news item appeared in the papers after the last blackout: "During the power failure many people complained of having gotten stuck for hours on escalators."

-Sam Levenson

*

Mr. Parker, for reasons unknown to him, received a bill from an oil company for several consecutive months for $0.00. He laughingly showed the bills to friends and waited for the bills to stop coming. When he got one marked "Final Notice," however, plus a threat to turn the account over to a notoriously tough collection agency, he wrote out a check for no dollars and no cents, signed his name, and mailed it to the oil company with a note saying, "This pays my account in full." Darned if he didn't get a form letter thanking him for his patronage.

-Bennett Cerf

*

This may be the age of technology, but some things never change. A woman came home late from work one night and found that her husband was still out. By eleven, she was getting worried, since he wasn't at his office, so she called five of his friends, got five answering machines, and left the same message on all five before she went out looking for him herself. "John's not home," she said on each machine. "Is he staying the night with you?"

When she got back at 2:00 A.M., there were five messages on her answering machine. Every one of them said, "Yes, John's spending the night with me."

*

The trouble with the world today is that when we give up that hour in April, no one feels sure we'll get it back in the fall.

*

Now our beaches are unsafe. All over New Jersey this summer, you could hear parents threatening their kids: "Shut up or I'll make you go play on the beach!"

*

Did you hear about the new Italian birth-control method? Garlic.

*

One prom chaperone to another as they watch the students gyrating: "I think these new dances are vulgar and horrible!"
"Yes, I agree. I can't do them, either."

*

One Indian to another: "Let's go on the warpath."
Second Indian: "We can't. It's being paved."

*

The husband comes home from work, tosses his briefcase into the closet, then sneaks up on his wife, who's scrubbing the kitchen sink. "Darling," he mutters, "let's go out and have some fun this evening."
"I'd love to, dear," she replies. "Only this time, leave the front light on if you get home before I do."

*

Money

The tourist's car had totally bogged down in the spring mudhole that the map called an "unimproved road." Luckily, a farmer appeared around the bend with his tractor, took the ten dollars offered to him, and towed the tourist onto firmer ground.

"You could make a good living pulling people out of this mudhole day and night," the tourist remarked as he prepared to leave.

"Nope," said the farmer. "Night's when we put the water on the road."

*

The farmer, justifiably proud of his horse, took it to the state fair to enter it in the judging. When he arrived, he tied his horse with all the others, then went to a nearby tent for a bite to eat. While the farmer was gone, two horse thieves stole into the livestock area; one of them made off with the horse while the other stayed behind to collect the tack.

Just then, the farmer returned from lunch to find his horse gone and the second thief standing in its place holding the horse's bridle and looking very sad.

"Sir," the quick-thinking thief said, " you are witnessing a miracle. Several years ago, I was living a sinful and wicked life. As punishment, I was turned into a horse — the one you bought and came to love. But now my punishment is over, if you will agree that I've been a good horse and set me free."

"I'll be danged," the farmer replied. "Well, you was the best horse I ever had. Take your freedom and go. You earned it."

Several weeks later, the farmer attended a fair in a neighboring state, where he saw his former horse for sale — in the form of a horse. He checked its teeth, looked at all the markings, and decided it really was his old horse, so he whispered into the horse's ear, "Son, you've got to learn to control yourself! I'll buy you one more time, but next time you ask, I'm saying no."

*

The federal agent knocked on the door of the old backwoods cabin and found himself greeted by a ragged little boy about six years old.

"Where's your father, son?"

"At the still."

"And your mother?"

"She's with him."

"Tell you what. I'll give you five dollars if you'll take me up to them."

"Okay," the boy said, holding out his hand for the money.

"No, I'll pay you when we get back."

"You'll pay me now, mister. You ain't coming back."

*

The unfortunate businessman had spent his entire adult life going into and recovering from bankruptcy. On his death, a note was found in his desk that stipulated six area bankers as his pallbearers. The note concluded, "These gentlemen carried me all my life. Let them finish the job."

*

"May the blessings of God follow you all the days of your life!" the woman beggar cried as the businessman stopped by her and reached into his pocket. When he pulled out a cigar and lit it up, she continued, "And never catch you!"

*

What's the difference between valor and discretion? Not passing out holiday tips to your doorman, super, and elevator operator is valor. Moving before the first of the year is discretion.

*

It's getting harder and harder to make ends meet these days. I was out walking in the woods the other day when I heard two snakes talking behind a rock. One said to the other, "If times don't get better soon, we won't have a spot to hiss in."

*

Monsters

Baby Kong to Daddy: "What's this thing I just caught, Daddy?"
"That's an airplane, son."
"How do I eat it?"
"Just like a peanut. Crack it open and eat what's inside."

*

What do you get if you cross a vampire with a parrot? I don't know, but you'd better have some crackers in the house!

*

The vampire went for an airplane ride. "Would you like to see the menu, sir?" the stewardess asked.
"No, thank you. Just show me the passenger list."

*

What does the Loch Ness monster eat? Fish and ships.

*

"Mommy, why do all the kids say I look like a werewolf?"
"Shut up and brush your face."

*

Why was the vampire driving so slowly on the highway? He was looking for a major artery.

Politics

The campaigning Democrat was interrupted time after time by a man in the back of the crowd who kept proclaiming loudly that he was a Republican.

"And why are you a Republican?" the politician finally asked.

"My father was a Republican and his father before him," the man yelled.

"Well, suppose your father and grandfather were fools. What would that make you?"

"A Democrat!"

*

Announcement at a Fourth of July celebration: "Senator Jones will now make a speech. Immediately afterward, we will have an egg-throwing contest."

*

"Suppose you were and idiot, and suppose you were a member of Congress. But I repeat myself."

-Will Rogers

*

The wife of one of our representatives shook him awake one night. "Jim, there's a robber in the house," she whispered. "Get up."

The representative mumbled in reply, "No, dear. In the Senate, yes. But not in the House."

*

If you have a feeble-minded citizen in your community, put him in the proper institution and cheerfully pay taxes for his support. Don't dodge the issue by sending him to Congress.

*

In 1846, Abe Lincoln was campaigning for a seat in the House of Representatives. Attending a revival meeting one day, he heard the preacher ask everyone who wanted to go to heaven to stand. Lincoln remained seated. Recognizing Lincoln, the preacher said, "If Mr. Lincoln does not want to go to heaven and escape hell, perhaps he will tell us where he does want to go."

Lincoln replied, "I am going to Congress."

*

Citizen: "I've heard a great deal about you."
Politician: "Possibly. But you can't prove any of it."

*

The angry politician sent the following letter to one of his critics: "Sir, my secretary, being a lady, cannot type what I think of you. I, being a gentleman, cannot even think it. You, being neither, will undoubtedly understand exactly what I mean!"

*

One of the town's leading citizens arrived home one evening to find a dead jackass in front of his house. He promptly called his Congressman in Washington to inform him of what he'd found, and the Congressman, furious at being bothered, yelled into the phone, "Just bury the jackass and stop bothering me!"

"Fine, Congressman," the constituent answered. "I'll be happy to bury the jackass."

"Why did you even bother to call me about this?" the Congressman inquired.

"I was about to bury the jackass when it occurred to me that it was only decent to inform his relatives of his death."

*

Publishing

An Associated Press headline sent on the wires to radio, TV stations, and newspapers across the country: THIS YEAR'S DROUGHT IN THE NORTHEAST COMES 20 YEARS AFTER THE SAME REGION SUFFERED THRWORDS.

A few minutes later the AP sent the following correction: THIS YEAR'S DROUGHT IN THE NORTHEAST COMES 20 YEARS AFTER THE SAME REGION SUFFERED THRTIES.

-John Bohannon

*

A New York paper reported on Theodore Roosevelt's inauguration: "It was a scene never to be forgotten when Roosevelt, before the Chief Justice of the Supreme Court and a few witnesses, took his simple bath."

*

Then there was the time a New York paper transposed the headlines of its obituary and transportation columns and many decent but departed citizens were listed under the headline: PASSED THROUGH HELL GATE TODAY.

*

A local newspaper printed an article in which the following statement appeared: "Mr. Sean O'Reilly is a new defective on the police force."

In the following issue, to correct the error, the paper announced: "Mr. Sean O'Reilly is a new detective on the police farce."

*

Two literary agents were comparing authors over lunch one day. "Well," said one, "it's finally happened. One of my authors decided today, after ten years of writing, that he has absolutely no talent."

"So is he quitting?" asked the second agent.

"Good heavens, no! He's had far too many best-sellers to do that!"

*

Publisher to novice author: "I predict a most successful career for you. You write beautifully, your characters are clearly delineated — and you have a filthy mind."

-Bennett Cerf

*

A British newspaper once reported: "The duchess smashed a bottle of champagne against the ship, and amid the cheers of the crowd, slid on her greasy bottom into the sea."

Put Downs

A too jovial bear of a man was running for mayor and strode through a hall greeting everybody as a long-lost friend. One individual he clapped on the back with a hearty, "Surely, I've seen that face before."

"Very likely," agreed the voter. "I've been a guard at the county jail for the past thirty years!"

-Bennett Cerf

*

P. D. Armour, the head of the famous meat packing company, told the employees of one department that they could each order themselves a suit and have the bill sent to him. No price limit was set, so one young man decided to do it up well and bought himself an expensive set of evening clothes. When the bill came in, Armour sent for the man, checked to see the bill was accurate, then noted: "I wish to say to you that I have packed a great many hogs in my time, but I never dressed one before."

*

The headwaiter backed up two steps in horror as the young man swaggered up in his leather jacket, torn jeans, and motorcycle boots.

"Say, man, where's the rest room?"

"Go down the hall, turn left, and you'll see a sign that says Gentlemen," the waiter sniffed. "Don't pay any attention to the sign — walk right in, anyway."

*

The outlaw came through the swinging doors with both handguns ready for action. "All you lazy bums get out of here!" he yelled. Immediately the room emptied, except for a lone Englishman sipping his tea at a table in the back.

"Well?" yelled the outlaw. "Didn't you hear me?"

The Englishman slowly looked around the empty room. "Certainly, my good man. My, there were a lot of lazy bums in here tonight, weren't there?"

*

The young man had left the small country town some years before, gone to Hollywood, and become a movie and television star. Now, moderately famous and very rich, he decided to visit his backwater hometown to show its citizens how far he had come.

He pulled up to the local garage in his stretch limo and got out to smile at the citizens while his driver filled the car. Most of those walking by simply nodded in reply to his smiles, although some local boys sidled up to check out the car. No one seemed to recognize the young man, who was beginning to think his visit was a mistake.

Firally George, the gas station owner, appeared from under a broken-down car. He smiled in recognition, wiped his hands off on an oily rag, and walked over to shake hands. "Hello, Tom. Going away?" he asked cheerfully.

*

The visiting Englishman tossed a coin to his American host. "My great, great uncle was made a *lord* by the king on this shilling," he boasted.

The American snorted, rummaged through his pockets, and passed the Englishman a nickel. "My great, great grandfather was made an *angel* by the Indian on this coin."

*

On leaving a dull Hollywood party, Groucho Marx commented to his hostess: "I've had a wonderful evening, but this wasn't it."

*

"I'd like two medium-rare lamb chops — make sure they're not overdone — the baked potato with sour cream and chives — be sure it's hot — and a crisp, dry salad with French dressing. Oh, and waiter, make the chops lean."
"Yes, madam. Which way?"

*

The conductor on the evening commuter train entered the car wearing a sad face. "I'm sorry to have to tell you all that the station in Stamford has just burned to the ground."
"So?" came a voice from the back of the car. "By the time *this* train gets to Stamford, they'll have a new station built!"

*

"Will you have the steak or the Salisbury steak, sir?"
"What's the difference?"
"About two days, sir."

*

The two comedians had been jibing at each other for over a year, getting laughs at each other's expense, hurling insults left and right. One evening they chanced to meet at a Hollywood party. Everyone present stood back and fell silent, waiting for the verbal battle to begin. One of the comedians looked around and commented, "It looks like we're expected to engage in a battle of wits."
"No," the second comedian replied, "I wouldn't think of picking on an unarmed man."

*

"I've got an idea!" exclaimed the freshman.

The professor wearily replied, "Be kind to it. It's a long way from home."

*

"You're so conceited! You think you're great, don't you?"
"No, but what's my humble opinion against hundreds of others?"

*

"She's lying, you know?"
"How can you tell?"
"Her lips are moving."

*

He's so conceited they'd have to pin his ears back to get him through the Grand Canyon.

*

Dad was giving Junior one of his Abe Lincoln lectures. "When he was your age, Lincoln walked seven miles to school — each way."
"Yes, sir. And when he was your age, he was President of the United States."

*

The judge was instructing the jury in certain points of law, most of which were not to the defendant's benefit. The lawyer for the defense rose to exclaim, "Your Honor, if that's the law, I'll burn all my law books!"
To which the judge replied, "It might be better if you'd read them."

*

Religion

The college president had just dedicated an expensive sign for the campus entrance, which was immediately stolen by the senior class and hidden away. After searching for several days, the president found the sign and hid it elsewhere, then informed the senior class that unless the sign were returned by that Saturday night, they would all lose their privileges. That Sunday, he appeared in chapel before the glum and unsuccessful seniors and read the morning's text: "A wicked and adulterous generation seeketh for a sign and there shall be none given unto them."

*

Mrs. Clare Boothe Luce, well-known playwright and wife of the late publisher of *Time*, became a Catholic in middle life and had, of course, all the enthusiasm of the convert. Under President Eisenhower, she was appointed ambassador to Italy, and while she was there (an apocryphal story goes), a reporter once spied her in earnest conversation with the Pope.

It occurred to him that the conversation between Pope and ambassador might have enormous news value, and he drifted closer in an attempt to overhear.

He finally made it, and the first words he heard were those of His Holiness, saying in accented English, "But you don't understand, Mrs. Luce. I already *am* Catholic."

-Isaac Asimov

*

An earnest little girl was asked if she could repeat the week's memory verse. "I sure can. I even know its zip code: Luke 19:10."

*

Kids in Sunday school are often asked to memorize passages from the Sermon on the Mount, and a little girl proudly recited it like this for her family: "Blessed are the poor in spirit, for theirs is the kingdom of heaven. Blessed are they that mourn: for they shall be comforted. Blessed are the meek: for they shall ... they shall ... they shall come home, dragging their tails behind them."

*

A famous evangelist, in an unfamiliar town for a revival, asked a local boy how to get to the post office.

"Down two blocks, then one to the left," the boy replied.

"Thank you," said the evangelist. "Do you know who I am?"

"Nope."

"I'm a famous preacher. And if you come to hear me tonight, I'll show you the way to heaven."

"Oh, yeah?" the boy said doubtfully. "How can you do that when you don't even know the way to the post office?"

*

Different people look for different things in the Ten Commandments. Some are looking for divine guidance, some for a code of living, but most people are looking for loopholes.

-Sam Levenson

*

The meek shall inherit the earth, but how long will they stay meek after they get it?

-Sam Levenson

*

Our pastor's sermons are like the peace of God. They surpass all understanding.

-Sam Levenson

*

A detested old harpy finally gave up the ghost after snarling at everybody in town for eighty years. Just as the funeral services ended, a sudden storm blew up. There was a blinding flash of lightning followed by a terrific clap of thunder. From the group of soaked mourners came a voice: "Waal, she's GOT there!"

-Bennett Cerf

*

A wise old bishop in Virginia once urged a newly elected Congressman to go out in a pouring rain and cast his eyes heavenward. "It will bring a revelation to you," he predicted.

The Congressman did as bidden, and came back soaked to the skin. "Look at me," he wailed. "I didn't get any revelation. I only felt like a blithering idiot."

"Not bad," chuckled the bishop. "Don't you think that was quite a revelation for a first try?"

-Bennett Cerf

*

Late one rainy afternoon, when he saw no other customers inside, Mr. Finkelstein walked into an elegant but not kosher delicatessen. He bought some tomatoes, and, with elaborate insouciance, asked (for the first time in his life),"By the way, eh, how much costs that— bacon?" Came a terrific flash of lightning and clap of thunder. Finkelstein looked up to the heavens, protesting, "I was only *asking!*"

-Leo Rosten

*

Two bellhops were discussing the best tippers in the hotel.

"Watch out for that preacher's convention," cautioned the older bellhop.

"Are they cheap?" asked the younger man.

"Let me put it this way," answered the voice of experience. "Last year they showed up with the Ten Commandments in one hand and a ten-dollar bill in the other, and when they left, they hadn't broken either."

-George Jessel

*

"I really do love Henry," wailed June, "but I could never marry an atheist! Why, he doesn't believe in anything — not even in hell."

"Don't you worry, dear," soothed her mother. "You marry him, and we'll convince him."

-George Jessel

*

Getting inoculated with small doses of religion prevents people from catching the real thing.

-Sam Levenson

*

You say you don't go to services because "the place is full of hypocrites"? Don't let that bother you. There's always room for one more.

-Sam Levenson

*

If God seems so far away — who moved?

-Sam Levenson

*

Show Business

Anytime I watch one of those awards shows that seem to go on forever, I end up feeling they should shoot fewer movies and more actors.

*

Did you know Sampson and Delilah put on the first successful vaudeville show in history? Brought the whole house down.

*

Hotshot actor: Anytime I perform, the people in the audience are glued to their seats.
Wife: Whatever works for you, dear.

*

Wife: This play's terrible! Why do you keep applauding like that?
Husband: To keep myself awake, dear.

*

"She has a leading part in the movies, you know?"
"She's a star?"
"No. Head usher."

*

Sports

Moses and Saint Peter took a day off from heaven in order to indulge themselves with an invigorating game of golf.

Moses, stepping up to the first tee, surveyed the course with a practiced eye and, addressing the ball, sent it screaming down the fairway. He watched it roll onto the green with a certain smugness.

Wordlessly, he made way for Saint Peter who, a bit chagrined, hit the ball forcefully, too, but, alas, hooking it in his haste. From the curved nature of the trajectory, it appeared certain to disappear into the woods. Moses was smiling even more smugly, but at the last moment, an eagle made its appearance from nowhere.

The great bird snatched the ball just as it was about to disappear into the foliage forever and then, with powerful beatings of its pinions, made its way to the green. It circled downward in a tight spiral and, five feet from the ground, let go of the ball, which dropped neatly into the hole.

And Moses said, "Look, Pete, you want to play golf, or you want to fool around?"

-Isaac Asimov

*

Rabbi Korshak, the young, modern rabbi in a suburban temple, greatly loved to play golf. He played as often as he could, usually with members of his congregation; but he took his pastoral duties so seriously that he could not find time to play more than four or five times a year.

One sunny Saturday morning, after services, Rabbi Korshak saw that his calendar was clear, and felt so powerful a craving to play golf, even if only for a few holes, that he begged God to forgive him for breaking the Sabbath, tossed his golf bag into the back of his car, and

91

sped off to a golf course a good thirty miles away, where he was certain no one would recognize him.

With an apology to his Maker on his lips, and a song of sixpence in his heart, the Rabbi teed off....

Up in heaven, Moses, looking down to earth, observing the ways and follies of Man, suddenly bolted upright. "Lord! My Lord!" he cried, "I beseech Thee: Gaze down. Do my eyes deceive me? There, Holy One — beyond those clouds — do you *see?*"

"Y-yes," said the Lord.

"That's Rabbi Korshak!" said Moses. "Playing *golf!* On Your Holy Sabbath!"

"Dear Me," sighed the Lord.

"Such a transgression!" said Moses. "From a rabbi yet. How will You punish him?"

"I," sighed the Lord, "will teach him a lesson."

And with that God cupped His hands over His mouth and — just as Rabbi Korshak teed off for the second hole — the Almighty One, King of the Universe, let out His breath in a long, mighty, cosmic **"Whoosh!"** that caught the rabbi's golf ball in midair, lifted it 300 yards, flipped it around a tree, over a stream and against a rock, where it ricocheted in a miraculous parabola to make — a hole in one!

Moses stared at God in bewilderment. *"That* you call a punishment, Lord?"

"Mmh," smiled the Lord. "Whom can he tell?"

-Leo Rosten

*

The baseball season's starting up and one team's really going in for training. Just hired four coaches — one for hitting, one for fielding, one for pitching, and one for Gillette commercials.

-Robert Orben

*

I was just reading about a ballplayer who was in such a bad slump that— he did a TV shaving commercial, took a swipe at his face — and missed!

-Robert Orben

*

Armstrong played a twosome on the golf course with the minister of his church one or two times a month. Reverend Brown was a good golfer and the competition between them was keen, but Armstrong had to admit that the matches offered a special strain on his internal workings.

Armstrong had, as so many of us do, a gift for rich invective, and on foozling a shot he had a habit of voicing his feelings by addressing the ball, the green, and the general surroundings with a wealth of purple passion. Yet in the presence of Reverend Brown, he found himself restrained from indulging himself, and by the end of the round he would be pale with repressed verbiage.

The minister, on the other hand, though he also foozled shots now and then, would on such occasions observe a patient silence that irritated Armstrong.

Finally, Armstrong said, "Reverend Brown, I must ask — Tell me, how is it you manage to keep your temper when you slice the ball into the rough, or when you miss your putt because there's a twig on the green you didn't see?"

Reverend Brown replied, "My good friend, it is a matter of sublimation. I need not shout or use vile language. Surely that will not alter the situation and will, on the other hand, imperil my soul. Yet since I must do something, I sublimate. I spit!"

"You spit?"

"That's right." Here, Reverend Brown's eyes darkened. "But let me tell you this! Where I spit, the grass never grows again!"

-Isaac Asimov

*

An avid golfer went to a fortune teller with a burning question: "Does heaven have golf courses? Can I play golf in the afterlife?"

Gazing deeply into her crystal ball, the fortune teller mumbled a little under her breath and said, "I have good news and bad news. The good news is that there *are* golf courses in heaven. In fact, they are beyond belief. There are no crowds and no bugs. The courses are perfectly maintained, with expert caddies and the finest equipment you can imagine."

"Wow! That's wonderful!" exclaimed the golfer. "But what's the bad news?"

"You're scheduled to tee off next Saturday morning."

*

Boy, the Meadowlands Stadium is vast. Why'd they go and give it to such a half-vast team?

*

Mabel threw herself across the doorway, blocking Martin's path. "Not this Saturday, Martin. You're staying home and mowing the lawn, not golfing."

"Move aside, Mabel. I tee off in half an hour."

"Martin, if you go golfing today, I'll knock your block off!"

"Hah! You wouldn't even know which club to use!"

*

Most people address a golf ball twice: Once before they swing and once after.

*

"Caddy, why do you keep looking at your watch?"

"This isn't my watch. It's a compass."

*

94

The angler looked up from the stream and spoke to the man sitting above him on the bank. "You've been sitting there watching me fish for two hours now. Why don't you just fish yourself?"

"Ain't got the patience for it."

*

One night I heard a lion prowling around the camp, coming closer and closer to my tent. No one else heard him, and I knew he'd kill me if I didn't kill him first, so I sneaked out of the tent and shot him in my pajamas. How he got into my pajamas I'll never know.

*

Stinginess

Did you hear about the man who found a package of cough drops one day? He was so stingy, he made his wife sleep without a blanket so she'd catch a cold.

*

Then there's the tightwad who pulled his kids out of school when he heard they'd have to pay attention.

*

Or the man who punished his son for buying an all-day sucker at 4:00 P.M.?

*

Then there's the woman married to a tightwad who actually enjoyed herself when the stove blew up during dinner — it was the first time they'd been out of the house together in twenty years.

*

Told by his service that he had an emergency prescription to fill, the druggist hurried to his store in the middle of the night and found the stingiest man in town waiting out front.

"My doctor says I should take this," the man said as he handed a note to the druggist.

"Ten cents worth of bicarbonate of soda? You woke me up for this when a glass of hot water would do about as much good?"

"A glass of warm water?" said the customer, taking the note back from the druggist. "Thank you for the advice, and have a good night."

*

Students

The teacher noticed little Billy flipping a coin while taking a true-or-false test. "What are you doing, Billy?" she asked.

"Taking the test, teacher. Heads is true, tails false."

Just before the end of the period, after almost everyone had turned in their papers, the teacher noticed Billy was flipping the coin again. "What are you doing now, Billy?"

"Checking my answers."

*

"If I lay one egg here and another over there, how many eggs will I have, Johnnie?"

"Teacher, I really don't think you can do it."

*

"Henry, if you had two apples and your brother asked you for one, how many apples would you have left?"

"My big brother or my little brother?"

*

"Teacher, I think I should warn you to watch out for my dad."

"Why, Tommy? Your father's a nice man."

"Yes, but he told me that if my grades didn't improve soon, someone was going to get a licking."

*

"Oh," little Sammy moaned, "it's in the cards that I'm getting a licking tonight."

"That's stupid, Sammy," said Pete. "Nobody can tell the future by using cards."

"My mom can. She'll take one look at this report card and tell me exactly what'll happen to me when Dad gets home."

*

Teacher: "Johnnie, use the word vermin in a sentence."
Johnnie: "Before I go fishin' I go vermin'."

*

The nursery-school teacher had spent a half hour dressing her charges for their outdoor playtime, pulling on boots, zipping jackets, matching mittens. As she finished struggling with Mary's boots, she let out a sigh of relief.

Then Mary tapped her on the arm. "These boots aren't mine, teacher."

With a groan, the teacher kneeled down and pulled off Mary's boots. "Do you know whose boots these are, Mary?"

"Sure. My sister's. Mom makes me wear them, though."

*

"George, please tell the class what a synonym is."
"A synonym means the same thing as the word you can't spell."

*

A friend of mine received the following letter from his son, the college freshman.

Dear Dad,

I'm sorry I haven't called or written to you in so long, but my one phone call I had to use to call the lawyer, and they only allow us to write one letter a month here. At least now I have a private room with good food and plenty of time to study. My lawyer says I should be out in time for summer vacation, with good behavior.

The girl I met at the freshman mixer may call you someday soon. She said something about needing money for the delivery, and I referred her to you. You'll really like her. She's the star of our freshman play, and plans to support me and the baby through a career on the stage. Personally, I plan to major in something a little more practical. Right now, I'm all wrapped up in basket-weaving, and hope to make a career out of it.

Love, John

P.S. Dad, I'm not really in jail, and I didn't even go to the freshman mixer. But I did fail calculus and got a D in Spanish, and I wanted you to be in the proper frame of mind for that news! See you at Christmas.

*

Texas

They really do things big down in Texas. They've got an auto showroom in Dallas three acres wide and wall-to-wall with Cadillacs, Lincolns, Imperials. And over in one corner, there's this little pile of Volkswagens with a placard: **Take one**.

-Robert Orben

*

I just heard of an Alaskan who wants to visit Texas, but he's afraid to. Suffers from claustrophobia.

*

Texas and Alaska are always competing to see who's the biggest, the richest, the best. If they'd work together, it would help them both. Alaska would be a great place to live if the air was a little warmer, and who has more hot air than Texas?

*

You know what I think hurts Texans the most? The thought that if we ever split Alaska in two — Texas'd be the *third* largest state.

-Robert Orben

*

A Texan and a New Yorker met in neutral territory at 30,000 feet. Finding himself with a captive audience, the Texan boasted, "You want to see progress, come visit me in Dallas. We're building so fast out there that it only takes us a week to build a thirty-story office building."

"That's nothing," replied the New Yorker. "I saw them laying the cornerstone of a building on my way to work one day. On my way home that night, the landlord was already evicting tenants for not paying their rent."

*

The Texan was a little awed by the ruins of the European cathedral, but he wasn't about to admit that to anyone. "How long did it take to build this place?" he asked the guide.

"Five hundred years, sir."

"Five hundred years! Why in Texas we could build one of these and have it turn to ruins in two or three years!"

*

The Texan decided to visit Alaska and see what all the fuss was about. "Sure, the place is big," he later admitted to his neighbors. "I even had a run-in with a bear up there. Even though I had a rifle with me and emptied it into him, he still kept coming at me. I ran for the nearest tree, but the lowest branch was *thirty feet* above the ground. Just as I was getting ready to jump for it, the bear swung at me and ripped my pants. Scared me so badly I totally missed the tree limb!"

"What happened?"

"Caught it on my way down."

*

Transportation

When an El Al plane leaves New York, the pilot greets the passengers in these words: "*Sholem Aleichem,* ladies and gentlemen, and welcome to El Al airlines. This is your pilot, Itzchak Levin, wishing you a happy, restful trip, which we certainly expect to have, God willing. And if by some remote chance we do run into trouble — God forbid! — do not panic, keep calm. Your life belt is under your seat. And if you must put it on, wear it in the best of health!"

-Leo Rosten

*

An Orion Airways chartered jetliner had taken off with one hundred passengers, taking them to a vacation on the Greek island of Crete. Takeoff was on time and smooth, and minutes later at cruising altitude of thirty thousand feet, the pilot's voice came over the intercom.

"This is the captain speaking. Sorry, but we are returning to the Birmingham Airport. We forgot the luggage."

-John Bohannon

*

One hot summer night at the drive-in, all was quiet as the movie's hero attempted to land his damaged plane in an open field. Suddenly the movie's control tower called out, "All you people in cars line the field and turn on your headlights. *Now!*"

Immediately, the drive-in was flooded by the headlights of over one hundred parked cars.

*

What a car! I'm gonna call it Flattery, 'cause it gets me nowhere! I wouldn't call it expensive. Let's just say it's the kind of car that can keep you strapped without seat belts. I won't say the car is old, but it's the first time I ever saw bifocal headlights.

-Robert Orben

*

My car's so old, it has orthopedic brake shoes.

*

"What will it cost to have this car fixed?" the woman asked the mechanic.

"What's wrong with it?"

"I haven't the faintest idea."

"Then it'll be two hundred fifty-six dollars."

*

"What would your wife say if you went out and bought yourself a new car?"

"Same old stuff: Don't drive so fast...Watch out...Use the turn signal...Wipe your feet!"

*

Dad went out to inspect Junior's "new" car. After climbing under it, into it, and over it, he wiped off his hands and gave his verdict: "Son, you've got a fine rearview mirror here. Why don't you jack it up and run a car under it?"

*

" Were you in complete control of the car at the time of the accident?" the judge asked the defendent.

"No, Your Honor. My wife was with me."

*

Travel

Aunt Maud arrived at her nephew's front door in an awful state, exhausted, sweaty, and out of breath. "Aunt Maud!" the nephew exclaimed. "You look terrible! What happened to you?"

"I just walked all the way from the airport, that's what's wrong with me!" Aunt Maud sputtered. " You said it was just a hop, skip, and a jump from your house, but it must be miles."

"It is. About five miles, as a matter of fact."

"How's that a hop, skip, and a jump, then?"

"Well, I expected you to hop into a cab, skip the five mile walk, and jump out here!"

*

What do you call all the little rivers feeding the great Nile River? The Juveniles.

*

Tour guide to gorgeous blonde: "Do you like old ruins?"
Blonde: " I certainly do. I married that one being helped onto the bus, didn't I?"

*

Two middle-aged cruise ship passengers were leaning on a railing trying to impress each other with their knowledge of life at sea. "What would you do if a storm suddenly appeared on the starboard?" the first asked the second.

"Throw out an anchor," the second replied.

"What if another storm sprang up to your aft?"

"Throw out another anchor."

"And if one suddenly appeared dead ahead?"

"Another anchor."

"Wait a minute! Where are you getting all these anchors?"

"Same place you're getting all your storms."

*

The mother, thinking things were a little too quiet, even for a vacation at a lake, found her husband snoring in a chair. "Where's Jimmy?" she asked, shaking him awake.

"Well, if he knows as much about canoes as he thinks he does, he's out canoeing. But if he doesn't know as much as he thinks, he's out swimming."

*

Waiters

Is there stew on the menu today, waiter?"
"No, sir. I wiped it off."

*

"Do you serve crabs here, waiter?"
"Have a seat. We serve anyone who comes in."

*

"What's the difference between the regular meal and the blue-plate special, waiter?"
"The regular meal is two dollars more, sir."
"Why? Is the food better?"
"No, but we do wash the plate."

*

"Waiter, does the chef have pig's feet today?"
"I don't know, sir. He has his shoes on."

*

"Waiter, the chicken I had yesterday didn't have a wishbone."
"Ah, but it was a happy chicken, madam. It had nothing to wish for."

*

"Waiter, look at this chicken! It has one long leg and one short leg."
"Do you intend to eat it or dance with it, sir?"

*

"Waiter, this meal isn't fit for a pig!"
"I'm sorry, sir. Let me take it back and bring you one that is."

*

WASPs

After the stock market fell so much, the following definition went around Wall Street: *What's the difference between a Yuppie and a pigeon?* A pigeon can still make a deposit on a BMW.

*

Why do bees wear yarmulkes? So people won't think they're WASPs.

*

Wise Guys

The Martian landed in Las Vegas and wandered into a casino just as a slot machine was paying off a super jackpot. The extraterrestrial went up to the one-armed bandit as it spewed out hundreds of coins and said, "If I were you, I'd stay in bed with a cold like that!"

*

High over the Alps, an airplane — carrying the pope, a famous soap-opera leading man, and a boy scout — caught on fire. The pilot, who was no hero, put on the first parachute he could find, told his passengers there were only two chutes left, and bailed out, leaving them short one parachute.

"It pains me, but I must take one of the chutes," said the actor. "People all over the world admire me, and millions of women adore me. I am the greatest actor in the world." Just before jumping, he looked at the other two and intoned, "I must do this for my fans. Farewell!"

Time was running out, so the pope said to the boy scout, "My child, I've had a good long life, and my faith tells me the next world will be a better place than this. You are young and have everything ahead of you. Take the remaining chute with my blessing."

"Not to worry, Your Holiness," the boy said, "Mr. Vanity just bailed out with my knapsack on his back!"

*

A gangster and his moll are walking down the street when she spots a beautiful fur coat in a store window. "Oh, I love that coat," she purrs to her companion.

Without batting an eye, the gangster picks up a brick, smashes the display window, retrieves the fur, and drapes it over her shoulders.

A short time later, they pass a jewelry store. " Oh, I'd love that diamong ring," the lady coos, admiring a rock the size of Gibraltar.

Without saying a word, her hero picks up a brick, smashes the window, plucks the precious stone from the debris, and places it on her dainty finger.

They walk a little farther and she catches sight of a brand-new Jaguar gleaming in a showroom, then leans up to whisper in the gangster's ear, "Oh, I'd love to own that beautiful car!"

Her boyfriend stops, turns around, and snaps, "Hey, whatdaya think, I'm made of bricks?"

*

An old miser was heading for the big bank vault in the sky, so he called his oldest and dearest friends to his bedside: his minister, his doctor, and his lawyer.

"Listen," he gasped, "don't tell me I can't take it with me, because I'm going to, with your help. I'm entrusting each of you with an envelope containing ten thousand dollars in cash. Wait until they're lowering my casket into the ground, and at the last possible moment, throw the money in with me."

It was a strange request, but when the dark day arrived, the three friends were in attendance. After the service, they got together to talk about the departed.

"I have a confession to make," the minister said sadly. "Our church's day-care center needed a new heating system, so the envelope I tossed in only contained seven thousand dollars cash. I'm so ashamed of myself."

"If it makes you feel any better, I wasn't entirely honest, either," added the doctor. "There's a little free clinic downtown that desperately needed repairs on its X-ray machine. I only threw in six thousand in cash."

"I can't believe you guys!" said the lawyer, shaking his head. "You violated a sacred trust. I, of course, threw in the entire amount — in the form of my personal check!"

*

Sir Edmund had always dreamed of being the first to scale the dreaded snow-covered volcano high in the Andes. The treacherous mountain's reputation was so daunting that even the most experienced adventurers avoided it, but Sir Edmund was determined to conquer the peak on his own.

The first three thousand feet were child's play. At eight thousand, he had passed the highest point ever reached by climbers. At fourteen thousand, he was within a half day's climb of the summit.

Suddenly, the ground shook violently as the volcano erupted and sent a cubic mile of hot lava spewing in all directions. The shock-waves knocked Sir Edmund off his feet just as the side of the mountain gave way. Sir Edmund tumbled over the edge of the volcano, six thousand feet above the bubbling magma.

As he was falling, he instinctively reached out and grabbed a small tree — barely more than a twig, really — sticking out of the side of the mountain. Losing his British reserve, Sir Edmund cried out, "Oh, God! If there's anyone up in heaven, help me!"

The answer came in a voice even deeper than the volcano's: "Sir Edmund, the most important thing is to have faith. You must believe what I say. Let go of the branch."

Sir Edmund glanced down into the bubbling cauldron of magma more than a mile below him, then looked back up to the sky. "I say, Old Man, by any chance is there someone else up there I can talk to?"

*

At the end of the auction, the auctioneer announced, "Just one more item of business. We've been informed that someone in the room has lost a wallet containing ten thousand dollars in cash. He is offering one hundred dollars for its return."

Just then, a voice from the back of the room called out, "One hundred and ten!"

*

Word Play

Every morning, rain or shine, the fisherman would go to sea, and each night he would tell his family of the tremendous fish he had seen and had almost caught.

This fisherman had two sons of whom he was very proud. One was named Toward, and the other was named Away.

One morning he took his sons fishing with him for the first time. That night when he returned, he was more excited than ever. "Listen," he told his wife, "you should have seen the tremendous fish we saw today. It was five feet long, and it crawled right up on the beach. But before I could do anything, it grabbed Toward and swallowed him in one gulp."

"Oh, that's terrible!" his wife said. "Poor Toward!"

"But that's only part of it," the fisherman said, holding his head. "You should have seen the one that got Away!"

*

Long, long ago an old Indian chief was about to die, so he called for Geronimo and Falling Rocks, the two bravest warriors in his tribe. The chief instructed each to go out and collect buffalo skins. Whoever returned with the most skins would be the new chief. About a month later, Geronimo came back with one hundred pelts, but Falling Rocks never returned. Even today as you drive through the West you can see signs saying: **Watch Out for Falling Rocks.**

*

Two Jewish *k'nockers,* approaching Honolulu, got into an argument about the correct pronunciation of Hawaii: One was sure it was Hawaii, the other positive it was Havaii. They made a bet.

When they got off the plane, they hurried over to the first native they saw and said, "Aloha! How do you pronounce the name of this island: Hawaii or Havaii?"

"Havaii," said the native.

"Thank you."

"You're velcome," said the native.

-Leo Rosten

*

If a one L-lama is a Tibetan holy man and a two L-llama is the South American version of a camel, what's a three L-lllama? One heck of a fire!

*

Did you know that Cher has an identical twin sister? Their mother named them Cher and Cher Alike.

*

The old medicine man was holding a group of dude-ranch guests entranced with tales of the Old West. "Greatest brave of all was Cherokee named Shortcake. A great bear had been attacking members of his tribe, so Shortcake went into forest alone to hunt the killer. Three days and three nights passed before rescue party found Shortcake and the bear. They had both died in the battle. Shortcake was a hero, so they brought his body back to his wife."

"What happened then?" a tenderfoot asked.

"Easy, kid," smiled the old man. "Squaw bury Shortcake."

*

On a remote South Sea island, the natives were all members of a cargo cult that worshipped the strange artifacts abandoned by our troops after World War II. The most revered objects of all were the strange thrones that dotted the ruins of the base. Since the chairs were thought to possess magical powers, the native chief ordered them all gathered up and hidden in the attic of his hut. One night during a typhoon, the ceiling collapsed and buried the chief under thousands of pounds of toilets.

Moral: People who live in grass houses shouldn't stow thrones.

*

Two boll weevils came to town to make their fortunes. One worked hard and eventually became rich and famous. The other was always lazy, so he remained the lesser of two weevils.

*

Work

Tombstone engraving is one of the oldest and kindest art forms in the world. Since epitaphs are, in essence, hand-carved letters of recommendation to God, they are almost invariably flattering. In the stonecutter's trade, the men who write those glowing tributes to the deceased are called "monumental liars."

-Sam Levenson

*

The young hardware-store clerk was amazing. He not only had a photographic memory that allowed him to keep everyone's accounts straight in his head, he knew exactly how many of each item were in each bin and what each had cost the store owner. He was also honest and hard working— a true find.

But one day the devil appeared to the store owner and told him he had come for the young clerk. "No, I can't possibly spare him," the owner complained.

"Sorry, but it's time."

"There must be some mistake. He shouldn't be yours, even if it is his time. Look, I'll make a deal with you. If you can fool him, you can take him. If not, he stays here."

So the devil found the clerk behind the counter and asked him, "Do you like eggs?"

"Yes, sir," the boy replied. The devil vanished. The boy continued to work at the store, growing into a man, marrying his boss's daughter, and fathering three sons who showed every sign of being as brilliant as their father.

One day as the man was balancing the store's books in his head, the devil reappeared in front of him again. "How?"

"Fried," the man answered with a smile. The devil disappeared in a puff of smoke, never to return to the little hardware store again.

*

It was a sweltering day on the Mediterranean, and the inside of the massive wooden ship was filled with the groans of the slave rowers. Whips were cracking like static electricity when the head galley-slave beater came in with news for the oarsmen.

"I've got good news and bad news, slaves. The good news is that I've ordered an extra ration of gruel for each of you at supper. The bad news is, the captain wants to go water skiing!"

*

The new DPW worker was complaining to his foreman on the first day of work. "I don't have a shovel. Everyone else on the crew does."

"Hey, if you don't have a shovel, you can't dig. Why're you complaining?"

"Because I don't have anything to lean on like the other guys do."

*

The clerk in the unemployment office was surprised by the lady next in line to apply for benefits, especially since she was wearing designer clothes and a huge diamond ring. But he had a job to do. "Occupation?" he asked.

"I toil not," the woman answered. "Neither do I spin."

Grunting in reply, the clerk wrote, "Lily of the field."

*

The magician and his parrot were entertaining the passengers of an ocean liner one evening. After making the parrot disappear and reappear, the magician set the parrot's cage off in the wings and went on with his act. First he made a chair disappear and reappear, then a small boy from the audience. Just as the boy reappeared, the ship struck an iceberg, split in two, and sunk. A few minutes later, the magician and parrot were alone in the water, both clinging to the same piece of wood. "Okay, wise guy," the parrot squawked, "now let's see you bring it back!"

*

Knock knock.
Who's there?
Abbot.
Abbot who?
Abbot you don't know who this is!

* * *

Knock knock.
Who's there?
Abe Lincoln.
Abe Lincoln who?
Dummy! Don't you know who Abe Lincoln is?

* * *

Knock knock.
Who's there?
Ach.
Ach who?
God bless you!

* * *

Knock knock.
Who's there?
A cheetah.
A cheetah who?
A cheetah never wins.

* * *

Knock knock.
Who's there?
Adam.

Adam who?
Adam up and get the total.

* * *

Knock knock.
Who's there?
Adele.
Adele who?
Adele is where the farmer's in.

* * *

Knock knock.
Who's there?
Adore.
Adore who?
Adore is between us. Open up.

* * *

Knock knock.
Who's there?
Agatha.
Agatha who?
Agatha feeling you're fooling.

* * *

Knock knock.
Who's there?
Ahead.
Ahead who?
Ahead is on your shoulders.

* * *

Knock knock.
Who's there?
A herd.
A herd who?
A herd you were home, so I came over!

* * *

Knock knock.
Who's there?
Aida.
Aida who?
Aida sandwich at recess time.

* * *

Knock knock.
Who's there?
Akron.
Akron who?
Akron give you anything but love, baby.

* * *

Knock knock.
Who's there?
Alaska.
Alaska who?
Alaska no questions. You tella no lies.

* * *

Knock knock.
Who's there?
Alby.

Alby who?
Alby glad when school's over.

* * *

Knock knock.
Who's there?
Alfred.
Alfred who?
Alfred the needle if you'll sew the button on.

* * *

Knock knock.
Who's there?
Ali.
Ali who?
Ali Bama.

* * *

Knock knock.
Who's there?
Alison.
Alison who?
Alison to the radio.

* * *

Knock knock.
Who's there?
A little boy who can't reach the doorbell.

* * *

122

Knock knock.
Who's there?
Allmen.
Allmen who?
Allmen act silly.

* * *

Knock knock.
Who's there?
Allotta.
Allotta who?
Allotta noise you're making.

* * *

Knock knock.
Who's there?
Althea.
Althea who?
Althea in my dreams.

* * *

Knock knock.
Who's there?
Amos.
Amos who?
A mosquito bit me.

* * *

Knock knock.
Who's there?
Andy.
Andy who?

And he bit me again.

* * *

Knock knock.
Who's there?
Andrew.
Andrew who?
Andrew a picture of me today.

* * *

Knock knock.
Who's there?
Anita.
Anita who?
Anita minute to think it over.

* * *

Knock knock.
Who's there?
Annette.
Annette who?
Annette is needed to catch butterflies.

* * *

Knock knock.
Who's there?
Annie.
Annie who?
Annie-body seen my lost dog?

* * *

Knock knock.
Who's there?
Apollo.
Apollo who?
Apollo you anywhere if you blow in my ear!

* * *

Knock knock.
Who's there?
Apricot.
Apricot who?
Apricot my key. Open up!

* * *

Knock knock.
Who's there?
Archer.
Archer who?
Archer mother and father at home?

* * *

Knock knock.
Who's there?
Arthur.
Arthur who?
Arthur mometer is broken.

* * *

Knock knock.
Who's there?
Aster.
Aster who?

Aster yourself.

* * *

Knock knock.
Who's there?
Astor.
Astor who?
Astor if she kept a diary.

* * *

Knock knock.
Who's there?
Atom.
Atom who?
Atom N. Eve.

* * *

Knock knock.
Who's there?
Attack.
Attack who?
Attack is sharp if you sit on it.

* * *

Knock knock.
Who's there?
Augusta.
Augusta who?
Augusta wind blew my hat off!

* * *

Knock knock.
Who's there?
Avenue.
Avenue who?
Avenue knocked on this door before?

* * *

Knock knock.
Who's there?
Avon.
Avon who?
The Avon lady. Your doorbell isn't working.

* * *

Knock knock.
Who's there?
Ax.
Ax who?
Ax your mother if you can come out and play.

* * *

Knock knock.
Who's there?
Banana.
Banana who?
Knock knock.
Who's there?
Banana.
Banana who?
Knock knock.
Who's there?
Banana.
Banana who?

127

Knock knock.
Who's there?
Orange.
Orange who?
Orange you glad I didn't say banana again?

* * *

Knock knock.
Who's there?
Bay.
Bay who?
Bay be face, you've got the cutest little baby face!

* * *

Knock knock.
Who's there?
Be.
Be who?
Be down to get you in a taxi, honey.

* * *

Knock knock.
Who's there?
Beckon.
Beckon who?
Beckon goes well with eggs.

* * *

Knock knock.
Who's there?
Ben.
Ben who?

Ben down and tie my shoes, please.

* * *

Knock knock.
Who's there?
Ben Hur.
Ben Hur who?
Ben Hur waiting for ten minutes.

* * *

Knock knock.
Who's there?
Bob.
Bob who?
Bob, baa black sheep, have you any wool?

* * *

Knock knock.
Who's there?
Boo-hoo.
Boo-hoo who?
Boo-hoo-hoo.
Boo-hoo-hoo who?
Boo-hoo-hoo-hoo.
Boo-hoo-hoo-hoo who?
Boo-hoo-hoo-hoo-hoo.
Boo-hoo-hoo-hoo-hoo who?
Stop it! You're breaking my heart!

* * *

Knock knock.
Who's there?

Boop-boopie.
Boop-boopie who?
Boop-boopie doo.

* * *

Knock knock.
Who's there?
Butch, Jimmy, and Joe.
Butch, Jimmy, and Joe who?
Butch your arms around me, Jimmy a kiss, or I'll Joe home.

* * *

Knock knock.
Who's there?
Butcher.
Butcher who?
Butcher feet on the floor.

* * *

Knock knock.
Who's there?
Butter.
Butter who?
Butter be home before midnight.

* * *

Knock knock.
Who's there?
Butternut.
Butternut who?
Butternut try to pick up a skunk.

* * *

Knock knock.
Who's there?
Bwana.
Bwana who?
Bwana hold your hand.

* * *

Knock knock.
Who's there?
Caesar.
Caesar who?
Caesar jolly good fellow.

* * *

Knock knock.
Who's there?
Cameron.
Cameron who?
Cameron film are what you need to take pictures.

* * *

Knock knock.
Who's there?
Candy.
Candy who?
Candy door be opened? I want to get out.

* * *

Knock knock.
Who's there?

Canine.
Canine who?
Canine, B-6, O-74. BINKO!

* * *

Knock knock.
Who's there?
Canoe.
Canoe who?
Canoe help me with my homework?

* * *

Knock knock.
Who's there?
Canoe.
Canoe who?
Canoe come out and play with me?

* * *

Knock knock.
Who's there?
Cantaloupe.
Cantaloupe who?
Cantaloupe without a ladder.

* * *

Knock knock.
Who's there?
Carfare.
Carfare who?
Carfare a cookie or a piece of pie?

* * *

Knock knock.
Who's there?
Carmen.
Carmen who?
Carmen get it.

* * *

Knock knock.
Who's there?
Cartoon.
Cartoon who?
Cartoon ups are necessary to
keep your car running smoothly.

* * *

Knock knock.
Who's there?
Catch.
Catch who?
Gesundheit!

* * *

Knock knock.
Who's there?
Catsup.
Catsup who?
Catsup a tree.

* * *

Knock knock.

Who's there?
Cayuse.
Cayuse who?
Cayuse your bathroom?

* * *

Knock knock.
Who's there?
Celeste.
Celeste who?
Celeste time I'll tell you a knock-knock joke.

* * *

Knock knock.
Who's there?
Celia.
Celia who?
Celia later.

* * *

Knock knock.
Who's there?
Chaise.
Chaise who?
Chaise him away.

* * *

Knock knock.
Who's there?
Chester.
Chester who?
Chester minute and I'll see.

* * *

Knock knock.
Who's there?
Choo-choo train.
Choo-choo train who?
Choo-choo trained the lion, but he had trouble getting the tiger to cooperate.

* * *

Knock knock.
Who's there?
Closure.
Closure who?
Closure mouth, I'm talking!

* * *

Knock knock.
Who's there?
Cock-a-doodle.
Cock-a-doodle who?
Are you a rooster?

* * *

Knock knock.
Who's there?
Colin.
Colin who?
Colin here, shut the window.

* * *

Knock knock.
Who's there?
Column.
Column who?
Column loud and clear.

* * *

Knock knock.
Who's there?
Consumption.
Comsumption who?
Consumption be done about these knock-knock jokes?

* * *

Knock knock.
Who's there?
Datsun.
Datsun who?
Datsun of mine is sure a little pest!

* * *

Knock knock.
Who's there?
Deboy.
Deboy who?
Deboy is cute.

* * *

Knock knock.
Who's there?
Deep.
Deep who?

Deep ends on who you were expecting.

* * *

Knock knock.
Who's there?
Della.
Della who?
Della Katessen.

* * *

Knock knock.
Who's there?
Dewey.
Dewey who?
Dewey have to listen to all this knocking?

* * *

Knock knock.
Who's there?
Dick.
Dick who?
Dick 'em up, I'm a tongue-tied rubber.

* * *

Knock knock.
Who's there?
Diesel.
Diesel who?
Diesel be your last chance to open the door.

* * *

Knock knock.
Who's there?
Dishes.
Dishes who?
Dishes me. Who ish you?

* * *

Knock knock.
Who's there?
Disjoint.
Disjoint who?
Disjoint is closed.

* * *

Knock knock.
Who's there?
Distress.
Distress who?
Distress hardly covers my knees.

* * *

Knock knock.
Who's there?
Divan.
Divan who?
Divan the bathtub — I'm drowning.

* * *

Knock knock.
Who's there?
Divan.
Divan who?

Divan the pool and go swimming.

* * *

Knock knock.
Who's there?
Doris.
Doris who?
Doris closed — that's why I knocked.

* * *

Knock knock.
Who's there?
Dozen.
Dozen who?
Dozen anybody want to let me in?

* * *

Knock knock.
Who's there?
Duke.
Duke who?
Duke the halls with boughs of holly.

* * *

Knock knock.
Who's there?
Duncan.
Duncan who?
Duncan doughnuts in your milk makes 'em soft.

* * *

Knock knock.
Who's there?
Dwayne.
Dwayne who?
Dwayne the bathtub, I'm dwowning.

* * *

Knock knock.
Who's there?
Dynamite.
Dynamite who?
Dynamite play with us if we're good.

* * *

Knock knock.
Who's there?
Eclipse.
Eclipse who?
Eclipse my hair in the barber shop.

* * *

Knock knock.
Who's there?
Edsall.
Edsall who?
Edsall there is — there isn't anymore.

* * *

Knock knock.
Who's there?
Egypt.
Egypt who?

Egypt me, call a cop.

* * *

Knock knock.
Who's there?
Egypt.
Egypt who?
Egypt me when he gave me change!

* * *

Knock knock.
Who's there?
Eileen.
Eileen who?
Eileen on a walking stick.

* * *

Knock knock.
Who's there?
Eileen.
Eileen who?
Eileen over to tie my shoes.

* * *

Knock knock.
Who's there?
Elder.
Elder who?
Elder in my arms all evening.

* * *

Knock knock.
Who's there?
Elephants.
Elephants who?
Elephants Gerald, the singer.

* * *

Knock knock.
Who's there?
Ellison.
Ellison who?
Ellison the alphabet after K.

* * *

Knock knock.
Who's there?
Emerson.
Emerson who?
Emerson big eyes you've got, baby.

* * *

Knock knock.
Who's there?
Ether.
Ether who?
Ether bunny.

Knock knock.
Who's there?
Hop.
Hop who?
Hop, hop way, Ether bunny gone.

Knock knock.
Who's there?
Cargo.
Cargo who?
Cargo beep and ran over the Ether bunny

Knock knock.
Who's there?
Boo.
Boo who?
Don't cry — Ether bunny be back next year.

* * *

Knock knock.
Who's there?
Etta.
Etta who?
Etta Kett.

* * *

Knock knock.
Who's there?
Eva.
Eva who?
Eva since yesterday I've been knocking.

* * *

Knock knock.
Who's there?
Eyewash.
Eyewash who?
Eyewash I had a million dollars.

* * *

Knock knock.
Who's there?
Fang.
Fang who?
Fang you very much.

* * *

Knock knock.
Who's there?
Ferry.
Ferry who?
Ferry tales can come true.

* * *

Knock knock.
Who's there?
Finish.
Finish who?
Finish it yourself.

* * *

Knock knock.
Who's there?
Fire engine.
Fire engine who?
Fire engine one and prepare for blast-off

* * *

Knock knock.
Who's there?
Formosa.

Formosa who?
Formosa the term I was absent from school.

* * *

Knock knock.
Who's there?
Freeze.
Freeze who?
Freeze a jolly good fellow.

* * *

Knock knock.
Who's there?
Gary.
Gary who?
Gary me back to old Virginny.

* * *

Knock knock.
Who's there?
Gibbon.
Gibbon who?
Gibbon take if you want to get along in the world.

* * *

Knock knock.
Who's there?
Gladys.
Gladys who?
Gladys Friday — how 'bout you?

* * *

Knock knock.
Who's there?
Gopher.
Gopher who?
Gopher your gun, Marshal!

* * *

Knock knock.
Who's there?
Gorilla.
Gorilla who?
Gorilla my dreams, I love you.

* * *

Knock knock.
Who's there?
Gretta.
Gretta who?
Gretta long, little doggie, gretta long.

* * *

Knock knock.
Who's there?
Habit.
Habit who?
Habit your way.

* * *

Knock knock.
Who's there?
Hair.

Hair who?
Hair today and gone tomorrow.

* * *

Knock knock.
Who's there?
Hallo.
Hallo who?
Halloween.

* * *

Knock knock.
Who's there?
Hank.
Hank who?
Hank E. Chief.

* * *

Knock knock.
Who's there?
Harry.
Harry who?
Harry up, it's cold out here.

* * *

Knock knock.
Who's there?
Hatch.
Hatch who?
God bless you!

* * *

Knock knock.
Who's there?
Heel.
Heel who?
Heel be right back.

* * *

Knock knock.
Who's there?
Heidi.
Heidi who?
Heidi Ho!

* * *

Knock knock.
Who's there?
Hence.
Hence who?
Hence lay eggs.

* * *

Knock knock.
Who's there?
Henrietta.
Henrietta who?
Henrietta worm that was in his apple.

* * *

Knock knock.
Who's there?
Holly.

Holly who?
Holly Louya.

* * *

Knock knock.
Who's there?
Honeydew and cantaloupe.
Honeydew and cantaloupe who?
Honeydew you love me? We cantaloupe now.

* * *

Knock knock.
Who's there?
Howl.
Howl who?
Howl it be if I come to your house today?

* * *

Knock knock.
Who's there?
Hugh.
Hugh who?
Hugh Mility.

* * *

Knock knock.
Who's there?
Hugo.
Hugo who?
Wherever Hugo, I go, too.

* * *

Knock knock.
Who's there?
Hume.
Hume who?
Hume do you expect?

* * *

Knock knock.
Who's there?
Humphrey.
Humphrey who?
Humphrey ever blowing bubbles.

* * *

Knock knock.
Who's there?
Idaho.
Idaho who?
Idaho my own name.

* * *

Knock knock.
Who's there?
I don't know. I didn't open the door yet.

* * *

Knock knock.
Who's there?
Imus.
Imus who?
Imus get out of this rain.

* * *

Knock knock.
Who's there?
Iona.
Iona who?
Iona new car.

* * *

Knock knock.
Who's there?
Ira.
Ira who?
Ira member Mama.

* * *

Knock knock.
Who's there?
Iran.
Iran who?
Iran all the way home.

* * *

Knock knock.
Who's there?
Ireland.
Ireland who?
Ireland you a quarter if you promise to pay me back.

* * *

Knock knock.

Who's there?
Isabel.
Isabel who?
Isabel out of order?

* * *

Knock knock.
Who's there?
Isadore.
Isadore who?
Isadore locked?

* * *

Knock knock.
Who's there?
Israeli.
Israeli who?
Israeli great to see you again.

* * *

Knock knock.
Who's there?
Ivan.
Ivan who?
Ivan to hold your hand.

* * *

Knock knock.
Who's there?
Ivan.
Ivan who?
Ivan working on the railroad, all the livelong day.

* * *

Knock knock.
Who's there?
Ivan.
Ivan who?
Ivan wanting to drop over.

* * *

Knock knock.
Who's there?
Ivy League.
Ivy League who?
Ivy League for every drop of rain that falls, a flower grows.

* * *

Knock knock.
Who's there?
Jacket.
Jacket who?
Jacket up if you've got a flat tire.

* * *

Knock knock.
Who's there?
Jess.
Jess who?
Jess little old me.

* * *

Knock knock.

Who's there?
Jose.
Jose who?
Jose, can you see, by the dawn's early light?

* * *

Knock knock.
Who's there?
Juicy.
Juicy who?
Juicy any ghosts in the haunted house?

* * *

Knock knock.
Who's there?
Juneau.
Juneau who?
Juneau the capital of Alaska?

* * *

Knock knock.
Who's there?
Kangar.
Kangar who?
You will find them in Australia.

* * *

Knock knock.
Who's there?
Karen.
Karen who?
Karen a bundle of bricks isn't much fun.

* * *

Knock knock.
Who's there?
Kay.
Kay who?
Kay sera sera.

* * *

Knock knock.
Who's there?
Kerch.
Kerch who?
Gesundheit!

* * *

Knock knock.
Who's there?
Ketchup.
Ketchup who?
Ketchup with me and I'll tell you.

* * *

Knock knock.
Who's there?
Ketchup.
Ketchup who?
Ketchup to her before she turns the corner.

* * *

Knock knock.

Who's there?
Kleenex.
Kleenex who?
Kleenex are prettier than dirty necks.

* * *

Knock knock.
Who's there?
Leggo.
Leggo who?
Leggo the door — I wanna come in!

* * *

Knock knock.
Who's there?
Lessen.
Lessen who?
Lessen here and I'll tell you a knock-knock joke.

* * *

Knock knock.
Who's there?
Lettuce.
Lettuce who?
Lettuce pray.

* * *

Knock knock.
Who's there?
Linda.
Linda who?
Linda me some money, please.

* * *

Knock knock.
Who's there?
Lion.
Lion who?
Lion on a cold slab can be deadly!

* * *

Knock knock.
Who's there?
Lion.
Lion who?
Lion down on the job, eh?

* * *

Knock knock.
Who's there?
Lionel.
Lionel who?
Lionel roar if you don't feed him.

* * *

Knock knock.
Who's there?
Litter.
Litter who?
Litter go.

* * *

Knock knock.

Who's there?
Little old lady.
Little old lady who?
I didn't know you could yodel!

* * *

Knock knock.
Who's there?
Lois.
Lois who?
Lois the opposite of high.

* * *

Knock knock.
Who's there?
Lyndon.
Lyndon who?
Lyndon Bridge is falling down.

* * *

Knock knock.
Who's there?
Major.
Major who?
Major ask, didn't I?

* * *

Knock knock.
Who's there?
Mandy.
Mandy who?
Mandy lifeboats — the ship is sinking!

* * *

Knock knock.
Who's there?
Marcella.
Marcella who?
Marcella's full of water. Call a plumber.

* * *

Knock knock.
Who's there?
Marsha.
Marsha who?
Marsha-mallow.

* * *

Knock knock.
Who's there?
Max.
Max who?
Max no difference. Let me in.

* * *

Knock knock.
Who's there?
Mayonnaise.
Mayonnaise who?
Mayonnaise have seen the glory of . . . .

* * *

Knock knock.

Who's there?
Me.
Me who?
Don't you know your name?

* * *

Knock knock.
Who's there?
Mecca.
Mecca who?
Mecca noise like a duck.

* * *

Knock knock.
Who's there?
Mississippi.
Mississippi who?
Mississippi and Mr. Sippy. Can we come in?

* * *

Knock knock.
Who's there?
Missy.
Missy who?
Missy-laneous.

* * *

Knock knock.
Who's there?
Monopoly.
Monopoly who?
Monopoly's bigger than your nopoly.

* * *

Knock knock.
Who's there?
Morris.
Morris who?
Morris Monday; next day's Tuesday.

* * *

Knock knock.
Who's there?
Moscow.
Moscow who?
Moscow gives more milk than Pa's cow.

* * *

Knock knock.
Who's there?
Mountie.
Mountie who?
Mountie horses and go for a ride.

* * *

Knock knock.
Who's there?
Mush.
Mush who?
Mush be twenty past eight.

* * *

Knock knock.

Who's there?
My panther.
My panther who?
My panther falling down. I need a belt.

* * *

Knock knock.
Who's there?
My Tommy.
My Tommy who?
My Tommy aches.

* * *

Knock knock.
Who's there?
Navajo.
Navajo who?
You'll Navajo until you open the door.

* * *

Knock knock.
Who's there?
Needle.
Needle who?
Needle little money for the movies.

* * *

Knock knock.
Who's there?
Newton.
Newton who?
Newton doing.

* * *

Knock knock.
Who's there?
Nicholas.
Nicholas who?
Nicholas half as much as a dime.

* * *

Knock knock.
Who's there?
Noah.
Noah who?
Noah good place to eat around here?

* * *

Knock, knock.
Who's there?
Nobody.
Thank goodness!

* * *

Knock knock.
Who's there?
Nobody. I'm just banging on the table.

* * *

Knock knock.
Who's there?
November.
November who?
November when we used to tell knock-knock jokes?

163

* * *

Knock knock.
Who's there?
Nunna.
Nunna who?
Nunna your business.

* * *

Knock knock.
Who's there?
Odyssey.
Odyssey who?
Odyssey a dentist if your tooth hurts.

* * *

Knock knock.
Who's there?
Olga.
Olga who?
Olga round to the back door.

* * *

Knock knock.
Who's there?
Olive.
Olive who?
Olive you, too, honey.

* * *

Knock knock.

Who's there?
Oliver.
Oliver who?
Oliver troubles will soon be over.

* * *

Knock knock.
Who's there?
Omen.
Omen who?
Omen river, O omen river.

* * *

Knock knock.
Who's there?
Orange.
Orange who?
Orange you ever going home?

* * *

Knock knock.
Who's there?
Orange.
Orange who?
Orange you glad I'm here?

* * *

Knock knock.
Who's there?
Orange.
Orange who?
Orange you glad there are knock-knock jokes?

* * *

Knock knock.
Who's there?
Orange juice.
Orange juice who?
Orange juice sorry you made me cry?

* * *

Knock knock.
Who's there?
Orson.
Orson who?
Orson wagon are parked outside.

* * *

Knock knock.
Who's there?
Osborn.
Osborn who?
Osborn down in Mississippi. Where were you born?

* * *

Knock knock.
Who's there?
Oscar.
Oscar who?
Oscar if she wants to go to the party.

* * *

Knock knock.

Who's there?
Oscar.
Oscar who?
Oscar if she loves me.

* * *

Knock knock.
Who's there?
Oswald.
Oswald who?
Oswald mah gum.

* * *

Knock knock.
Who's there?
Otto.
Otto who?
Otto know. I've got amnesia.

* * *

Knock knock.
Who's there?
Pasture.
Pature who?
Pasture math test, didn't you?

* * *

Knock knock.
Who's there?
Pecan.
Pecan who?
Pecan somebody your own size.

* * *

Knock knock.
Who's there?
Peeper.
Peeper who?
Peeper and salt, that's who.

* * *

Knock knock.
Who's there?
Pepper.
Pepper who?
Pepper up. She looks tired.

* * *

Knock knock.
Who's there?
Perry.
Perry who?
Perry Scope.

* * *

Knock knock.
Who's there?
Phil.
Phil who?
Phil 'er up with regular, please.

* * *

Knock knock.

Who's there?
Phillip.
Phillip who?
Phillup the tub so I can take a bath.

* * *

Knock knock.
Who's there?
Phyllis.
Phyllis who?
Phyllis in on the news.

* * *

Knock knock.
Who's there?
Phyllis.
Phyllis who?
Phyllis pitcher with water, please.

* * *

Knock knock.
Who's there?
Pocket.
Pocket who?
Pocket in the pocking lot.

* * *

Knock knock.
Who's there?
Police.
Police who?
Police hurry up. It's chilly outside.

* * *

Knock knock.
Who's there?
Police.
Police who?
Police may I sit down?

* * *

Knock knock.
Who's there?
Police.
Police who?
Police stop telling knock-knock jokes.

* * *

Knock knock.
Who's there?
Possum.
Possum who?
Possum ketchup for my hamburger.

* * *

Knock knock.
Who's there?
Pressure.
Pressure who?
Pressure shirt.

* * *

Knock knock.

Who's there?
Radio.
Radio who?
Radio not, here I come.

* * *

Knock knock.
Who's there?
Red.
Red who?
Red pepper. Isn't that a hot one?

* * *

Knock knock.
Who's there?
Rhoda.
Rhoda who?
Rhoda boat across da lake.

* * *

Knock knock.
Who's there?
Ripsaw.
Ripsaw who?
Ripsaw you downtown yesterday.

* * *

Knock knock.
Who's there?
Rita.
Rita who?
Rita good book lately?

* * *

Knock knock.
Who's there?
Robin.
Robin who?
Robin a coffin is dangerous.
You could be in grave trouble.

* * *

Knock knock.
Who's there?
Robot.
Robot who?
Robot Jon't splash with the oars.

* * *

Knock knock.
Who's there?
Roland.
Roland who?
Roland butter taste good.

* * *

Knock knock.
Who's there?
Ron.
Ron who?
Ron faster, there's a witch after us.

* * *

Knock knock.
Who's there?
Roseanne.
Roseanne who?
Roseanne the tulip are my favorite flowers.

* * *

Knock knock.
Who's there?
Roxanne.
Roxanne who?
Roxanne shells were on the beach.

* * *

Knock knock.
Who's there?
Saber.
Saber who?
Saber, she's drowning!

* * *

Knock knock.
Who's there?
Sahara.
Sahara who?
Sahara you today?

* * *

Knock knock.
Who's there?
Salmon.
Salmon who?

Salmon Jack are over at my house.

* * *

Knock knock.
Who's there?
Sam and Janet.
Sam and Janet who?
Sam and Janet evening, you will meet a stranger.

* * *

Knock knock.
Who's there?
Samoa.
Samoa who?
Samoa knock-knock jokes.

* * *

Knock knock.
Who's there?
Sandy.
Sandy who?
Sandy Claus!

* * *

Knock knock.
Who's there?
Santa Ana.
Santa Anna who?
Santa Ana gonna bring you anything
if you don't believe in him.

* * *

Knock knock.
Who's there?
Sarah.
Sarah who?
Sarah doctor in the house?

* * *

Knock knock.
Who's there?
Scold.
Scold who?
Scold enough to go ice-skating.

* * *

Knock knock.
Who's there?
Senior.
Senior who?
Senior uncle lately?

* * *

Knock knock.
Who's there?
Senior.
Senior who?
Senior so nosey, I won't tell you.

* * *

Knock knock.
Who's there?
Seymour.

Seymour who?
Seymour kittens out here.

* * *

Knock knock.
Who's there?
Shad.
Shad who?
Shad up and open the door.

* * *

Knock knock.
Who's there?
Sharon.
Sharon who?
Sharon share alike.

* * *

Knock knock.
Who's there?
Sherwood.
Sherwood who?
Sherwood like for you to let me in.

* * *

Knock knock.
Who's there?
Sherwood.
Sherwood who?
Sherwood like it if you'd let me kiss you.

* * *

Knock knock.
Who's there?
Sherwood.
Sherwood who?
Sherwood like to hear another knock-knock joke.

* * *

Knock knock.
Who's there?
Shirley.
Shirley who?
Shirley you must be joking.

* * *

Knock knock.
Who's there?
Socket.
Socket who?
Socket to me!

* * *

Knock knock.
Who's there?
Soda.
Soda who?
Soda you like me?

* * *

Knock knock.
Who's there?
Sofa.

Sofa who?
Sofa, so good!

* * *

Knock knock.
Who's there?
Sofa.
Sofa who?
Sofa you're doing fine.

* * *

Knock knock.
Who's there?
Somber.
Somber who?
Somber over the rainbow.

* * *

Knock knock.
Who's there?
Specter.
Specter who?
Specter Holmes of Scotland Yard.

* * *

Knock knock.
Who's there?
Spinach.
Spinach who?
Spinaching me so long I had to scratch it.

* * *

Knock knock.
Who's there?
Stan.
Stan who?
Stan aside — I'm coming through.

* * *

Knock knock.
Who's there?
Stella.
Stella who?
Stella nother crazy knock-knock joke.

* * *

Knock knock.
Who's there?
Sue.
Sue who?
Sue prize!

* * *

Knock knock
Who's there?
Summertime.
Summertime who?
Summetime itsa hot, summertime itsa cold.

* * *

Knock knock.
Who's there?
Summertime.

Summertime who?
Summertime I'm going to stop telling knock-knock jokes.

* * *

Knock knock.
Who's there?
Sum Toi.
Sum Toi who?
Sum Toi you've got there.

* * *

Would you know me if you didn't see me for a week?
Sure!
Would you know me if you didn't see me for a day?
Sure!
Knock knock.
Who's there?
See! You've forgotten me already.

* * *

Knock knock.
Who's there?
Swarm.
Swarm who?
Swarm enough to go swimming.

* * *

Knock knock.
Who's there?
Sweden.
Sweden who?
Sweden my tea with two lumps of sugar.

* * *

Knock knock.
Who's there?
Taffilda.
Taffilda who?
Taffilda bucket you have to turn on the water.

* * *

Knock knock.
Who's there?
Tamara.
Tamara who?
Tamara it's gonna rain.

* * *

Knock knock.
Who's there?
Tara.
Tara who?
Tara-ra-boom-de-ay!

* * *

Knock knock.
Who's there?
Tarzan.
Tarzan who?
Tarzan stripes forever.

* * *

Knock knock.

Who's there?
Telly.
Telly who?
Telly Phone.

* * *

Knock knock.
Who's there?
Thatcher.
Thatcher who?
Thatcher was a funny joke.

* * *

Knock knock.
Who's there?
Thermos.
Thermos who?
Thermos be someone waiting who feels the way I do.

* * *

Knock knock.
Who's there?
Thesis.
Thesis who?
Thesis a stickup!

* * *

Knock knock.
Who's there?
Thistle.
Thistle who?
Thistle make you whistle.